THEATRE SYMPOSIUM
A PUBLICATION OF THE SOUTHEASTERN THEATRE CONFERENCE

Gods and Groundlings: Historical Theatrical Audiences

Volume 20

Published by the

Southeastern Theatre Conference and

The University of Alabama Press

THEATRE SYMPOSIUM is published annually by the Southeastern Theatre Conference, Inc. (SETC), and by The University of Alabama Press. SETC nonstudent members receive the journal as a part of their membership under rules determined by SETC. For information on membership write to SETC, P.O. Box 9868, Greensboro, NC 27429-0868. All other inquiries regarding subscriptions, circulation, purchase of individual copies, and requests to reprint materials should be addressed to The University of Alabama Press, Box 870380, Tuscaloosa, AL 35487-0380.

THEATRE SYMPOSIUM publishes works of scholarship resulting from a single-topic meeting held on a southeastern university campus each spring. A call for papers to be presented at that meeting is widely publicized each autumn for the following spring. Authors are encouraged to send unsolicited manuscripts directly to the editor. Information about the next symposium is available from the incoming editor, David S. Thompson, Department of Theatre, Agnes Scott College, Decatur, GA, 30030, dthompson@agnesscott.edu.

THEATRE SYMPOSIUM
A PUBLICATION OF THE SOUTHEASTERN THEATRE CONFERENCE

Volume 20 2012

Contents

Introduction

E. Bert Wallace

MY INVOLVEMENT with the Southeastern Theatre Conference Theatre Symposium stretches back in some ways to its beginnings. The first Symposium conference was held in April 1992 with Dr. Philip G. Hill of Furman University as editor. I was a drama major at Furman under Dr. Hill, graduating in May of that year. That first conference was held at The University of Alabama at Tuscaloosa; the topic was "Commedia dell'Arte Performance." I later attended graduate school at Alabama under Dr. Paul Castagno, a commedia scholar and one of the founders of Theatre Symposium. Among my duties as Paul's harried graduate assistant were transcribing tinny audio recordings of the conference proceedings and implementing final changes for Volume 4 of *Theatre Symposium*, which Paul edited. My first scholarly presentation was at a Symposium. And, two decades after the first conference, I was named editor for Volume 20. The 2011 conference was held in April at Furman, with Dr. Hill (now a Professor Emeritus and "Phil" to me) serving as de facto host. It would have been difficult to imagine, as I sweated through Phil's theatre history and dramatic literature classes, where I'd be twenty years hence.

The 2011 topic, "Gods and Groundlings: Historical Theatrical Audiences," drew an interesting range of presenters and approaches. Of course, not every paper can be published (for a variety of reasons), but the presented papers not published in this volume deserve some mention. As a longtime fan of the theatre riot (I am fascinated by the Astor Place Riots, which I first learned about under Dr. Hill while at Furman, and was myself in a near-riot sparked by the apparent shredding of a live goldfish on stage while I was at Alabama), I was most pleased to hear several papers on audience violence: Sebastian Trainor (University of Washington) shattered my romantic notions about the Ubu Riots; Rick Jones (Stephen F. Austin State University) and Peter DuPuis dealt variously with Irish hooliganism in the theatre; and Wes D. Pearce of the University of Regina gave us a marvelous account of a Victorian-era riot involving the ladies of New York and a limited supply of free "Merry Widow" hats to be given away at a matinee. Other papers included a consideration of vaudeville and music hall audiences by former editor Susan Kattwinkel (College of Charleston); a discussion of producing and performing in a traveling Toby Show by Dawn Larson (Francis Marion University); an evaluation of Early Modern and contemporary audiences by Jeremy Fiebig (Fayetteville State University); and presentations by Sivan Grunfeld and Rayya El Zein, both of the CUNY Graduate Center. The papers published in this volume represent a similarly wide range.

This year's keynote speaker was Dr. Susan Bennett (University of Calgary), whose work (including the influential book *Theatre Audiences: A Theory of Production and Reception*) was cited by numerous presenters. In keeping with the spirit of the conference, Dr. Bennett attended all the sessions and held a conference response and discussion at the end of the event. Her insights were invaluable. Her paper is published in this volume as well.

One of the most valuable aspects of Theatre Symposium is the chance for scholars from all over the country (and often other countries as well) to learn from one another in an intimate setting with a single topic and no overlapping sessions. In addition to hearing everyone's work, we share meals, allowing discussions to continue and grow. Though the conference was organized into topical panels of two or three papers each, no attempt has been made to categorize the papers here. Rather, it is my hope that the value of a conference of scholars coming together to wrestle over a specific topic will be clear in the variety and quality of the papers published.

I must give special thanks to Phil Hill for his inestimable help—as editorial advisor, "leg man" at Furman, and, along with his wife, Margie, magnanimous cocktail-party host. Thanks also go to former editors J. K. Curry and Scott Phillips for all their help and support; Rhett Bryson of Furman University (another significant mentor from my undergraduate days) for regaling us all with his famous Laugh Lecture and including me in a relaxing morning of shop darts; Dr. Susan Bennett for agreeing to serve as keynote speaker and providing important insights and contributions to our discussions; Betsey Baun, Quiana Clark-Roland, and all the staff at the SETC Central Office for their support; Dan Waterman of The University of Alabama Press; Kat Redfern, our tireless student worker at Furman; Ran Whitley, Georgia Martin, and all my supportive colleagues at Campbell University; and finally to Kelley, Peter, and Betsy Wallace, whose support through many very early mornings and very late nights made this volume possible.

Making Up the Audience

Spectatorship in Historical Context

Susan Bennett

THE FIRST EDITION of my book *Theatre Audiences* (now some twenty years old) was motivated, at least initially, by work in the more literary field of reader-response theory. I had explored how that might be expanded and modified to capture reception practices that were both individual and collective and, significantly, public rather than private. But it was also very much part of my project to draw on a range of theatrical practices that extended far beyond the more usual terrain of theatre studies scholarship. So much academic discussion of theatre was grounded then in analysis of published play texts, of conventional dramas that had been, for the most part, originated on the main stages of New York and London, the premier theatre cities of the English-speaking world. Sometimes that scholarship showed little interest in what performance might actually bring to the words on the printed page. While *Theatre Audiences* drew on and developed from an existing body of criticism, as well as on the canon of dramatic literature as it was then taught in the university curriculum, the book also evolved from my own theatergoing experiences in the United Kingdom, the United States, and Canada—emphasizing the challenges, practices, and ideology of what we then called "alternative" theatres so as to promote my own idea of what Jacques Rancière would later call the "emancipated spectator."[1] My concern was with an audience that was at least as productive as the complex sign system comprising the onstage action.

The second edition of *Theatre Audiences,* published in 1997, extended that emphasis with the addition of a chapter on "intercultural" theatre, to account for an emergent interest in dramatic productions from outside the English-speaking world, particularly when they were imported for the pleasure of English-speaking audiences. This is an appetite that I would argue has since become even more voracious, so that audiences are now accustomed to performances of the familiar (say, a Shakespeare play) delivered in a non-Western performance tradition (say, Chinese opera) or in a language other than English. Often this is an equation that provides a production with a global market, appealing to audiences in many locations in the world: a recent example would be *Roman Tragedies* (a composite of Shakespeare's *Coriolanus, Julius Caesar,* and *Anthony and Cleopatra*) by Toneelgroep of the Netherlands that has been seen in several European countries as well as in North America. *Roman Tragedies* is performed in Dutch but with surtitles in the language of its local audience. Exposure to the conventions, styles, and assumptions of theatrical practices beyond an audience's usual horizon of expectations required a revision and expansion of the range of criteria for reception promoted in the first edition of the book. This is the scope that has, for the most part, characterized much of the scholarly work about audiences that has followed, my own included, so that the focus has been almost always on the contemporary, or at least very recent, moment. It is more than fair, then, that Ayanna Thompson, outlining her interest in spectatorship in the public theatres of Renaissance England, notes: "Like performance theory, reception theory aims to be universal but is actually tied to a modern historical and cultural moment."[2]

Even within that context of "a modern historical and cultural moment," there have been particular blind spots. So, when I was asked to revisit my theorization of the audience for a "state of the field" issue of *Theatre Survey* (November 2006), I wrote: "We have come a long way from imagining the universalized theatergoer watching a three-act play at a proscenium-arch mainstream theatre in London or New York, but we may not yet be expansive enough."[3] To this end, I referenced Claire Cochrane's critique of twentieth-century theatre history-making as overdetermined by scholars "whose highly selective narratives of the past derive from their own cultural and critical preferences. The experience of the past has effectively been filtered through the perspective of the critic-historian sitting as audience in her own favored performance environment."[4] Certainly, Cochrane's argument was intended to promote her own project, a recovery of amateur theatre in the first half of that century, but I repeat her objections here as a point of entry into the subject of this essay: historical audiences. If we have been so selective and limited in our interrogations of the recent past, or at least of the last hundred years or so, how can we appropriately and productively expand ideas of spectatorial expectations and practices to address a more remote historical past? As Thompson would have it, reception "is created through a complex amalgamation of the real and perceived histories of past performances,"[5] something I take as encouraging a more speculative and textured account of spectatorship.

The first and most pressing issue for any investigation of a historical audience is undoubtedly evidence. What do we know about the people who attended theatre in a specific period and geography? And, more broadly, what can we say about their taste? In the analysis of contemporary audiences, scholars tend to look to two kinds of evidence to make their case. Generally, evidence about what people thought about plays and performances comes in the form of reviews of specific productions, usually drawn from the mainstream press of the relevant city, and we often rely predominantly on the prose of a professional critic—a title that has meant different things, obviously, at different times but which at least implies an expert spectator with a vested interest in and acquaintance with professional theatrical experience. Feminist criticism, of course, has reminded us that reviewers for the "serious" daily newspapers have almost always been men, and that there have been gendered implications in what and how they review. As Susan Carlson curtly observed on the occasion of one particular account, "When a journalist like Robert Cushman reviews such an intensely feminist play as Sarah Daniels's *Masterpieces* with such unabashed sexism, there can remain no doubt that the relationship between women playwrights and the predominantly male community of reviewers is troubled."[6] It is also germane to ask what it means, for the matter of evidence, to review for remuneration. In general, as Helen Freshwater has trenchantly asked, "Theatre scholars cannot be unaware of these problems with reviews, so why do they continue to cite them?"[7]

Only very recently, in the explosion of Web-based resources and, specifically, blogging, has the amateur (and sometimes expert) reviewer provided a widespread and different order of evidence drawn from the "regular" theatergoer's view of a show.[8] Indeed, we have recently seen the remarkable crisis in reviewing produced by the seemingly endless preview period for the ill-fated Broadway musical *Spiderman: Turn Off the Dark* where a wealth of blog-based reviews circulating unanimously negative responses to the show led the main newspaper critics to overturn usual protocol and first review the show on one of the many nights it had been scheduled to officially open, even though it was in fact still a preview performance. This break with convention not only led, one assumes, to the firing of director Julie Taymor and a temporary end to previews while the show was rejigged, but also provoked a lively discussion about the role, responsibilities, and ethical obligations of the paid reviewer. Equally, the consistently negative reviews, amateur and professional (including those that followed the eventual official "opening night"), seem to have had little effect on actual audience response as the show continues to sell at ninety-five percent capacity in the 1,440-seat Foxwoods Theater, making the musical one of only five Broadway shows grossing more than $1 million a week.[9] As Freshwater notes in response to her own interrogation of the reliability and utility of reviews, "When dealing with theatre history, the answer is obvious: the written record—in the form of reviews—may be all that remains of the audience's reaction" and, as the *Spiderman* illustration suggests, it may be misleading to say the least.[10]

The other mainstay behind audience analysis is first-hand experience ("I was there"). Cochrane is surely right when she criticizes the critic-historian as limiting interest to "her own favored performance environment" (and admittedly *Theatre Audiences* was all about mine at that time). Coupled to this preference is, surely, a remarkably tenacious belief in "authenticity" of experience: the critic *knows* because the critic was there. The critic-historian not only writes about what she likes best but draws authority from that condition of having been there—an odd reliance on a fundamental "liveness," given the cautions that Phil Auslander has long attached to this term.[11] How this affects the production of theatre history is worth more discussion than it seems to have attracted to date, but suffice to mark here that for scholars writing about audiences outside their own theatergoing lifetimes, this predilection cannot be a problem. Rather, at the heart of any speculation about historically remote spectatorship is inevitably textual evidence from the period under scrutiny where typically we apply assiduous close reading strategies so as to discover explicit and implied audience engagements on which to base an argument about what those theatergoers expected, enjoyed, and sought out. This is bound to remain one of the potentially strongest sources of evidence. But, of course, a text is neither transparent nor secure as a source. On the one hand, for more or less any period we might care to approach, available play texts—especially if we mean by that one in a modern edition—will only ever represent a fraction of what was available to audiences for theatre in that particular historical moment. And what we have is either a blueprint for, or a record of, a performance (depending on a forward-thinking or an historically minded point of view): words on a page, a trace at best of the three-dimensionality of the stage. What we do not have are those plays, successful or not, that, whether for good reason or sheer bad luck, did not find their way to printed form, or that were printed but in too few copies or without careful enough preservation to exist however many years or centuries later for twenty-first-century scholars to consult. Other texts are ignored, misplaced, or miscataloged. But, even our interactions with an extant and readily available text are always mediated by the history of editing behind that text. This is something that scholars in Shakespeare performance criticism often note has a long history of editorial choices that promote the concerns of Shakespeare as poet and all-round literary genius rather than as a pragmatic man of the theatre. For this reason, editors have often been guilty of deleting, revising, or obscuring lines that have perfectly reasonable performance implications in favor of apparently improving the poetry or clarifying the plot.[12]

Alongside the print versions of play scripts, assumptions about spectators—their taste, their behaviors, their socioeconomic class, and so on—are often drawn from other contemporary writing about the theatre. So that Jeremy Lopez, in his book about theatrical convention and audience response in early modern drama, bases his argument on a wide selection of extant plays and on "antitheatrical writings from between the years of 1574 and 1642."[13] He writes "These writings [antitheatrical tracts] . . . represent the darker side of theatrical pleasure in the period, but the fact that they differ from protheatrical writings only in the estimation of the virtue of the tremendous hold plays could have over audiences, makes them a good index of the ways in which plays maintained this hold."[14] Either way, and in light of the limitations in contemporary reviewing practices, we need to reserve some skepticism about the reliability of this particular evidence.

Beyond the textual remnants of once-live performance and writing about the theatre in the same period, we have expected elements of theatre history to supplement this knowledge base. The size and architecture of a particular theatre, the concentration of performance spaces within an identifiable theatre district, as well as the cost of a theatre ticket are all aspects that we cite, whether investigating recent performances or those of long ago. What we want to know is who went to the theatre and how were they arranged when they did. These are areas that address ideas of social mobility, economic discretion, and hierarchies of viewing. Even when seemingly reliable evidence exists, processes of interpretation can yield wildly different accounts of spectator profiles. The first scholars to address the playgoer of Shakespeare's London—Alfred Harbage, Ann Jennalie Cook, and Andrew Gurr[15]—produced groundbreaking books with impressive original research, but their systems of description, especially of the differences between public and private theatres, were almost immediately challenged by other scholars whose own interests provided different vistas and engagements that would complicate the seeming distinctions that these books had drawn up. For example, Jean Howard, referring to both legal documents and antitheatrical texts, asserts that "ideological consequences of play going might be quite different for different social groups."[16] Howard continues:

> At the theater door, money changed hands in a way which enabled women access to the pleasure and privilege of gazing, certainly at the stage, and probably at the audience as well. . . . Whether or not they were accompanied by husbands or fathers, women at the theater were not "at home," but in public, where they could become objects of desire, certainly, but also desiring subjects, stimulated to want what was on display at the theater, which must have been, not just sexual opportunity, but all the trappings of a commodifying culture worn upon the very backs of those attending the theater and making it increasingly difficult to discern "who one really was" in terms of the categories of a status system based on fixed and unchanging social hierarchies.[17]

Speculation about audience behavior in the distant past relies, as we see here, in the productive confluence of contemporary interests (in Howard's case, the performativity of gender) with what we take as historical evidence (accounts of the presence of women in the audience). As much as in the contemporary framework assumed by my book *Theatre Audiences,* studies of audiences in earlier historical periods, like Howard's and Thompson's, have equally sought to emancipate particular subgroups from the assumptions of universal experience.

There is also a need to reexamine the centrality of particular playtexts upon which those theories have been determined, contested, and revised. Relevant, in this instance, is the fact that Lopez must establish in the introduction to his book on early modern spectatorship that he plans to work on "a great many plays" to uncover what audiences "enjoyed and experienced," suggesting "in this book, I will assume that plays that have been labeled as 'minor,' and have been condemned to relative obscurity, have the same kind of linguistic and dramatic complexity as the works of Shakespeare, and are worth looking at closely."[18] In other words, his examples draw on plays of the period that are seldom read and even less frequently performed, even though many of them were hugely successful on the seventeenth-century stage: this is the theatre of Francis Beaumont, Henry Chettle, John Day, and William Haughton and not (or not just) William Shakespeare, Thomas Middleton, and Ben Jonson. Likewise, Howard admits, in the epilogue to her *Theatre of a City:* "It is an ancillary benefit of this project that in exploring some of the resonant places of London comedy I have gotten to write about a number of plays not often examined in recent critical literature. For a long while Shakespeare has dominated the study of Renaissance drama,[19] and I have benefited from a long career happily writing about his plays and teaching them to my students. But the focus on Shakespeare changes the understanding we might otherwise have of the period and of the role of the drama in it."[20]

Indeed, in any historical period, what we promote as the "best" examples—the ones we regularly find in period and general anthologies (and we find the same plays, over and over again)—are generally no more than the tip of that period's iceberg of production, given particular value and importance often by way of literary rather than dramatic qualities and by virtue of repetition through dissemination in the classroom as much as other venues. So, even when we are well aware of a larger range of materials/evidence, there has been a remarkable willingness to stick with examples that are painstakingly well known. In a related vein, we need to remember that play texts assumed to constitute collectively a sufficient body of evidence may, in fact, present only a partial picture of what audiences chose to see.

Furthermore, the contextual theatre history that is so often deployed as an infrastructure for discussions of historical audiences tends, too, to be focused on the main venues in central locations (thus, for the early modern period, so often the Globe in London) with scant reference to the neighborhoods in which theatres are to be found and their relationship to other activities in the area. Howard's project, to elucidate "the process by which . . . plays helped to transform specific places into significant social spaces, that is, into environments marked by the actions, movements, and daily practices of inhabitants,"[21] suggests one strategy that I want to emphasize here as potentially productive to research about the historical audience. This is the relationship between place and performance. It is as relevant for audiences of the remote past as it is for those of a more contemporary time to ask whether the audiences were "of" the place where the performance was staged or whether they were drawn from a much wider geography. In her discussion of London, Howard writes that her subject plays did not simply "aim at giving audiences the pleasure of recognition. Rather, in invoking the places of the city and filling them with action, the plays also *construct* the city."[22] This is an important and viable assertion that accounts for a city—and a theatre industry—that was at that time expanding exponentially.

Similarly, in an article exploring the London city liberties, "urban spaces whose exemption from royal and mayoral jurisdiction allowed them to house criminals, prostitutes, and private theaters like Shakespeare's Blackfriars," Mary Bly looks at early modern London as "the ensemble of material, social, and symbolic codes that made up the social architecture of the city."[23] Both Howard's book and Bly's essay align, then, with the recent spatial turn in critical theory, an approach that recognizes the site-specificity of both texts and their audiences. This is crucial, I would argue, for a more engaged approach to the historical audience, to understand the social and cultural geographies to which performances and inhabitants both contribute.

To open up this speculation about the theatre audience yet further, we might draw on Richard Schechner's bifurcated definition for performance studies, a discipline invested in both what we understand "is" performance and what we see "as" performance ("what the object does, how it interacts with other objects or beings, and how it relates to other objects or beings"[24]). In the context of sixteenth- and seventeenth-century London, audiences for the theatre, irrespective of social class and level of education, were keenly attuned to performance culture across everyday life including public acts of torture and hangings, royal processions, and local festivals (the latter often preserving rituals and practices of a now residual Medieval theatricality). In other words, a spectator in the theatre was part of a knowing public that encountered a range of performances in their experience of place, whether in that theatre space or elsewhere across the city's landscape (or what Bly terms its "social architecture"). We may not have reliable data for the audiences of the period and thus have historically relied only on those few reviews and the notoriously overcited "antitheatrical" tracts to supplement a limited selection of plays, but recent scholarship has brought into view previously ignored performances, often site-specific and often by the period's leading figures, that suggest specific place-based spectatorial arrangements and distinctive audience composition.

In the field of early modern studies, ideas of place—what geographer Tim Cresswell would call "meaningful location"[25]—have emerged as an important matrix for thinking through the production and reception of plays. Perhaps not surprisingly, work to date has been predominantly concerned with public performances in urban environments and, thus, in the case of early seventeenth-century studies, almost always London and London only. Notwithstanding this singular focus, it is certainly worth paying careful attention to the theoretical imperatives of this scholarly work. Jean Howard's fascinating and important book *Theatre of a City* (2007) is especially provocative in the many ways it explores, to use her words, "the intimate synergy" she sees connecting London and the first commercial theatres there.[26] She writes: "each chapter of this book focuses on a particular place within the city and examines the way in which the stage created significant stories about it. The recurring features of plot and characters that structure these stories, and the changes rung on them over time, are crucial evidence of both the social tensions these plays helped to negotiate and the terms in which they made city space socially legible."[27] Of course, Howard draws her notion of social legibility from the work of Michel De Certeau (again, a theorist/philosopher concerned, primarily, with urban environment, evidenced by his oft-cited "Walking in the City"[28]). From this theoretical vantage point, she aims to investigate how "plays helped to transform specific places into significant social spaces, that is, into environments marked by the actions, movements, and daily practices of inhabitants."[29] What is important here, I think, is Howard's emphasis on the effects of these dramas, as performing spaces that rehearse, shift, and instate quotidian experience in the city. I'm interested, too, in her attention to how specific sites "become ideologically charged as they were visited and revisited by various dramatists and as they became connected with particular urban actors and with particular kinds of stories."[30] With this kind of perspective in mind, it is not surprising that Thomas Heywood's two-part *If You Know Not Me, You Know Nobody* has seen a flurry of recent critical interest, chiefly because the second of these plays enacts Thomas Gresham's building of the Royal Exchange in London and, as Charles Crupi has suggested, stages not just "admiration and respect for economic accumulation" in the city but simultaneously illuminates "the painful dependencies created by a market economy, the frank portrayal of poverty and the charity it inspires."[31] In other words, there was a pattern of plays, actors, and spectators connecting through the specificity of place-reference that not only produced meaning in the production of the drama but which extended into the actual physical spaces and their social contexts that the dramas both cited and explored.

Typically, then, studies of early modern theatre audiences—even when constrained to a single city location, London—have been concerned with a narrow band of theatergoing: it has been about playgoing in the public and private theatres of the late sixteenth and early seventeenth centuries. What I want to propose now, as a model for more comprehensive accounts of historical audiences, is an attentiveness to place-based analysis so as to identify specific sets of spectators as well as an extended framework in which to understand the dramatic output of a period. In the context of early modern performance, then, I will offer some examples premised on two interlocking factors: the first turns to what have heretofore been regarded as "minor" works by "major" figures and the second looks to move the discussion of audiences outside the theatre and, more crucially, outside London.

Ben Jonson's work has, of course, generated a long-standing and extensive critical bibliography almost all of which has been concerned with either his poetry or his plays for both boy and adult companies; indeed,

Bartholomew Fair (1614) might well be the most oft-discussed example of a site-specific London drama of the period. But few have considered his earlier work in the City of London; Jonson himself was apparently keen to bury that aspect of his vitae. Gabriel Heaton and James Knowles note that he "omitted his civic employments from his *Works* (1616)" even though Jonson had "early in his career . . . worked as a City pageant writer and as a provider of guild entertainments—as a kind of early modern party organizer."[32] Moreover, Jonson continued to provide performance work on commission, writing frequently for very specific audiences and in the context of a distinctive location. Heaton and Knowles's essay provides information about and discussion of Jonson's *The Merchant Taylors' Entertainment* (1607), an occasional piece with songs, designed specifically to entertain the eponymous guild and its distinguished guests—"most notably Prince Henry."[33] Composition of the guild membership (putatively the richest group in all the London guilds) and the complex relationship it would have had both to London's mayor and the court inflect any speculation about the entertainment's reception. As Heaton and Knowles explain, the mayor was refused an invitation to the evening because of his close relationship to another, competing guild, the Clothworkers, but showed up anyway with his aldermen.[34] Jonson's *Entertainment at Britain's Burse* (1609), only recently rediscovered (2004), was scripted to open London's New Exchange, a building intended to rival Gresham's Royal Exchange, and, as David Baker has observed, makes use of local elements such as "Shop Boy hawks" who would have been clustered in the immediate vicinity of the performance space.[35]

Other, later works by Jonson were commissioned for venues outside of London and thus extend, by way of country non-theatre spaces, evidence for and understanding of audience composition and engagement. *The King's Entertainment at Welbeck* was performed for Charles I on May 21, 1633, during his stopover with the Earl of Newcastle on a journey to Scotland. This work started with a sung dialog between "Doubt" and "Love" rendered as an accompaniment to a banquet dinner and later moved outdoors to Welbeck's park as a post-prandial diversion.[36] As Lisa Hopkins observes, Jonson's script mobilizes "many local references" and she further suggests that the "particular geographic locations" deployed in *The King's Entertainment at Welbeck* "produce a set of specificities whose connotations of inversion and hence misrule again work both to underline the importance of the local as opposed to the national perspective."[37] The emphasis on at least these two points of view (local/national) challenges the prevailing idea of the monarch as the singular implied audience and requires an equal imagination of other communities of spectatorship as well as a subdivision of that audience by location. Of course, the royal party would have seen all elements of the entertainment, but the later action in Welbeck's extensive park (that ran well in to Sherwood Forest, an already overdetermined site for English social relationships) would have been available to a wider group, not the least of which would have been the staff who were involved in preparing the horses that the royal party had intended to ride after dinner.

The King's Entertainment at Welbeck is but one of many dramas that Jonson wrote for locales other than theatre spaces, suggesting his sought-after talent for scripting site-specific performances that worked to deliver entertainment in a local context. The Earl of Newcastle was a repeat customer, commissioning another place-based project the year after *The King's Entertainment* and again to entertain Charles I on his travels. This time Jonson was asked to write for the setting of another of the Earl's properties; *Love's Welcome at Bolsover* was performed on July 30, 1634. Overall, these productions are suggestive of the importance given to place both for visiting and local components of the spectatorship.

A young John Milton also provided a script for performance outside London, on the occasion of the inauguration of John Egerton as the first Earl of Bridgewater and Charles's Lord President of the Council of Marches of Wales. This work has been, historically, best known as *Comus.* More recent scholarship has, however, asserted a return to its original title *A Maske Presented at Ludlow Castle* (indicative, then, of both genre and place) and a more accurate designation of coauthorship between Milton and Henry Lawes, the music tutor who was directly involved in the masque's production at the titular castle. Both shifts, among other things, remind us that this work, like those of Jonson, was intended for a specific audience, gathered at the Castle on Monday, September 29, 1634. The preference for identifying this work as Milton's *Comus,* by contrast, has been generally to suggest this as a "young" work by one of English literature's greatest poets, and to concentrate on this text for its attributes as poetry rather than have it appended to that altogether less prestigious genre of drama.

Indeed, there is a complicated textual history for this masque: it exists in at least three variants including one in Milton's hand (generally seen as a likely first version), a presentation copy (regarded as closest to what was performed), and one published three years after the date of the performance under Lawes's name.[38] But, instead of dwelling on Milton's work as text (either in the case of its three different versions or as poetry to be closely read), the recovery of its genre-based title returns this "evidence" to a performance history. Thinking about performance conditions at Ludlow and the demands on the masque's actors opens up the text for other seams of inquiry including possibilities for its reception. In collaboration with Julie Sanders, I have recently examined the site specificity of *A Maske* and, while I do not intend to repeat our argument in detail here,[39] the questions we raise about audience are germane to the project of the historical audience.

Milton is not known to have visited Ludlow at any time but rather furnished the preliminary script for the occasion. The music tutor, Lawes, appears then to have rehearsed the masque with its principal actors—the three children of John Egerton: Lady Alice (aged fifteen), John (eleven) and Thomas (nine). In other words, Lawes was responsible for adapting Milton's script both to the abilities of the young actors and to the occasion of their father's inauguration on site. We suggest, in this regard, that the masque moved between indoor and outdoor localities and that this generated two distinct audiences—one comprising the Bridgewater party and their guests who peripatetically witness the masque in its entirety and the other a local (citizen) audience that sees a different, shorter version (excluding participation in the pivotal banquet scene), one much more obviously focused on their preparation for the Earl's administration and exercise of power in the region. Among the Bridgewater audience, there is the embodied lesson for the children—their roles and responsibilities as they move toward adulthood—and for the Earl there is a blunt explication of the demands of governance: familial, regional, and, of course, on behalf of the King. Each of the audience's constituents has a lesson to learn, but how and where this is delivered as well as the specific content is remarkably nuanced through the manipulation of what we examine as site-specific performance. In other words, to think of a historical audience for this masque requires calibration of the particularities of the sites of performance and the accessibility of those places for particular constituencies of spectators. For *A Maske Presented at Ludlow Castle,* then, spectatorship is crafted both within and outside the text itself and this produces multiple possible engagements rather than a single thematic coherence for what has mostly been thought of as "Milton's *Comus.*" Rather, *Comus* is the history of a text that has been torn from its origins in performance to serve an entirely different critical enterprise; this action had effectively buried the very existence of its historical audiences. Part of the work for recovery of reception is to reexamine texts we might already know for evidence that expands and complicates what we know of theatrical production in the period under investigation.

Knotty problems emerge in any attempt to talk about historical audiences. What I hope I have illustrated here is, on the one hand, a need to interrogate those texts (both dramatic and related texts) that we accept as logical and significant evidence for whatever constructs of audience we might derive and, on the other hand, a need to examine evidence that falls outside—sometimes far outside—the usual range of material. What might seem to be esoteric, minor, or otherwise marginal remnants of the same historical moment can often not only redefine what we imagine constitutes appropriate evidence for our work but pose new and relevant questions that we might exercise on all the evidence before us. In this context, I have suggested that theatre history needs to pay more attention to theatre geography and that theatre buildings can only ever tell part of the performance story while play texts tell perhaps even less. What I want to encourage, then, is a creative skepticism around conventional ideas of evidence and a more animated practice of speculation—not just because the strategies should produce fuller accounts of spectatorship, but because they may also produce new ways of thinking about our old texts, invigorating not only critical theatre studies but a contemporary theatre practice interested in looking back at what audiences, sometimes a very long time ago and in many different places, obviously enjoyed.

Notes

1. Jacques Rancière, *The Emancipated Spectator,* trans. Gregory Elliott (London: Verso, 2009). Rancière's emancipated spectator is certainly different from my own, but both projects share an emphasis on activity over passivity; he suggests that spectators must "play the role of active interpreters, who develop their own translation in order to appropriate the 'story' and make it their own story. An emancipated community is a community of narrators and translators" (22).

2. Ayanna Thompson, *Performing Race and Torture on the Early Modern Stage* (New York: Routledge, 2008), 21.

3. "Theatre Audiences, Redux," *Theatre Survey* 47, no. 2 (November 2006): 228.

4. Claire Cochrane, "The Contaminated Audience: Researching Amateur Theatre in Wales before 1939," *New Theatre Quarterly* 19, no. 2 (May 2003): 169–70.

5. Thompson, *Performing Race,* 21.

6. Susan Carlson, *Women & Comedy: Rewriting the British Theatrical Tradition* (Ann Arbor: University of Michigan Press, 1991), 177.

7. Helen Freshwater, *Theatre & Audience* (Basingstoke: Palgrave, 2009), 36.

8. Some of the better-known examples include Kevin Daly's "The Theatre Aficionado at Large" (http://www.theatreaficionado.com/) (Daly is membership director for the Independent Theatre Bloggers Association—http://theaterbloggers.com/—which lists more than sixty members on its site), Jill Dolan's "The Feminist Spectator," a regularly published review blog that enacts the title of her landmark book, and "The Playgoer" (http://playgoer.blogspot.com/).

9. Information taken from BroadwayWorld.com, "Broadway Box Office Totals 11-06-05," http://broadwayworld.com/grosses.cfm. Kevin Flynn and Patrick Healy have pointed out, however, that operating expenses are running at $1.2 million a week and its box office gross around $1.2–1.3 million, less than the

percentage occupancy would suggest because many of the tickets are sold at discounted prices. See "How the Numbers Add Up (Way Up) for 'Spiderman,'" *New York Times,* June 23, 2011. http://www.nytimes.com/2011/06/23/theater/spider-man-by-the-numbers-breaking-down-its-costs.html.

10. Freshwater, *Theatre,* 36.

11. Auslander's *Liveness: Performance in a Mediatized Culture* was first published in 1999 (New York: Routledge); a second edition from the same publisher appeared in 2007.

12. For further discussion of this area, see Lukas Erne and Margaret Jane Kidnie's *Textual Performances: The Modern Reproduction of Shakespeare's Drama* (Cambridge: Cambridge University Press, 2004).

13. Jeremy Lopez, *Theatrical Convention and Audience Response in Early Modern Drama* (Cambridge: Cambridge University Press, 2007), 14.

14. Ibid.

15. Alfred Harbage, *Shakespeare's Audience* (New York: Columbia University Press, 1964); Ann Jennalie Cook, *The Privileged Playgoers of Shakespeare's London, 1576–1642* (Princeton, NJ: Princeton University Press, 1981); and Andrew Gurr, *Playgoing in Shakespeare's London* (Cambridge: Cambridge University Press, 1987).

16. Jean E. Howard, "Women as Spectators, Spectacles, and Paying Customers," *Staging the Renaissance: Reinterpretations of Elizabethan and Jacobean Drama,* ed. David Scott Kastan and Peter Stallybrass (London: Routledge, 1991), 70.

17. Ibid., 72–73.

18. Lopez, *Theatrical Convention,* 7.

19. As listed in note 15 above, all three book-length studies of the early modern audience specifically reference Shakespeare in their titles.

20. Jean E. Howard, *Theater of a City: The Places of London Comedy, 1598–1642* (Philadelphia: University of Pennsylvania Press, 2007), 215.

21. Ibid., 3.

22. Ibid., 23.

23. "Playing the Tourist in Early Modern London: Selling the Liberties Onstage," *PMLA* 122, no. 1 (January 2007): 61.

24. Richard Schechner, *Performance Studies: An Introduction,* 2nd ed. (New York: Routledge, 2002), 30.

25. *Place: A Short Introduction* (Malden, MA: Wiley-Blackwell, 2004), 7.

26. *Theatre of a City,* 2.

27. Ibid., 3.

28. Michel de Certeau, *The Practice of Everyday Life,* trans. Steven Rendall (Berkeley and Los Angeles: University of California Press, 1988), 91–110.

29. *Theatre of a City,* 3.

30. Ibid., 23.

31. "Reading Nascent Capitalism in Part II of Thomas Heywood's *If You Know Not Me, You Know Nobody,*" *Texas Studies in Literature and Language* 46, no. 3 (Fall 2004): 315.

32. "'Entertainment Perfect': Ben Jonson and Corporate Hospitality," *Review of English Studies* 54, no. 217 (2003): 587.

33. Ibid., 598.

34. Ibid. See especially 596–97.

35. "'The Allegory of a China Shop': Jonson's *Entertainment at Britain's Burse*," *English Literary History* 72, no. 1 (Spring 2005): 159–80.

36. Lisa Hopkins, "Play Houses: Drama at Bolsover and Welbeck," *Early Theatre* 2, no. 1 (1999): 27.

37. Ibid.

38. Detailed discussion of the textual variants can be found in *John Milton's Aristocratic Entertainments* by Cedric Brown (Cambridge: Cambridge University Press, 1995).

39. "Rehearsing Across Space and Place: Rethinking *A Maske Presented at Ludlow Castle*," *Performing Site-Specific: Politics, Place, Practice,* ed. Joanne Tompkins and Anna Birch (Basingstoke: Palgrave, 2012).

The Matinee Audience in Peril

The Syndicate's *Mr. Bluebeard* and the Iroquois Theatre Fire

Jane Barnette

When Oliver Wendell Holmes advised the court in 1919 that "the most stringent protection of free speech would not protect a man in falsely shouting fire in a theatre and causing a panic," his dictum was persuasive because it conjured a terrifying communal understanding of how dangerous (not to mention how common) theatre fires were. Of all the images that might arise in our public memory, however, there is only one that holds the title of the "worst theater fire in U.S. history"—the Iroquois Theatre fire of 1903.[1] There are several reasons to consider this calamity the worst of its kind. The fire (and the panic it caused) killed approximately six hundred patrons, about a third of the auditorium's capacity. Further, the horror of the Iroquois tragedy has less to do with magnitude than it does with context: because this fire started during a matinee performance, most of the spectators present (and thus, most of the victims) were women and children. Finally, not one person deemed responsible for the loss of so many lives was held responsible. All those initially charged were acquitted, and not one of the victims' families was compensated for damages or suffering.

Rather than relying on familiar approaches to live-audience scholarship, this paper will venture into the abyss of audience experience, anchored by the extant survivor narratives that were published in a frenzy of public memorial following the Iroquois disaster. Keeping in mind the sage warning from Dennis Kennedy that "almost anything one can say about a spectator is false on some level," I nevertheless wish to paint a portrait of the matinee spectator in order to hold this snapshot of reception up against the production that played while the fire burned.[2]

Significantly, the attraction that drew a record-breaking (and capacity-busting) audience to the opulent new Iroquois Theatre was the Theatrical Trust (or Syndicate)'s extravaganza *Mr. Bluebeard*. In the Bluebeard myth, the vicious title character methodically murders his wives and hides their dead bodies, warning each subsequent wife not to explore the basement where they are hidden. When each new wife goes against Bluebeard's wishes and enters the basement, she discovers a pyre of corpses that she will soon join, and the cycle begins again. The disturbing parallels between the fictional characters onstage and the rhetoric following the Iroquois disaster point to a shared understanding of the female spectator (whether as wife or patron) as *responsible* for her fate, given her "natural" curiosity and propensity to hysterics.

There is no doubt that the audience sought by this Syndicate-owned house was a female one, given its location and the nature of its threshold.[3] Located on the corner of Dearborn and Randolph Street (Chicago's equivalent to Broadway), the Iroquois Theatre was within strolling distance of the State Street department stores and boutiques that had begun to transform the Loop into a premier shopping destination by the turn of the twentieth century. As cultural historians have noted, "the feminization of State Street . . . gave the illusion of safety to middle-class city and suburban women and children,"[4] a perception that was made all the more visible by the increased foot patrol of police officers in this part of Chicago. On average, one hundred thousand passengers per day traveled to the Loop, most of whom made a day of shopping, lunching at a tearoom, and/or taking in a matinee performance at one of the many theatres on Randolph Street. As a journalist noted in 1904, because the Iroquois was built "nearest State Street, [with] the imposing entrance, sixty feet high, leading into a brilliantly decorated lobby, [the Iroquois] is expected to catch many strangers before they get further up the street."[5] The foyer was sumptuously designed with marble and mahogany, with grand staircases on either side of a wide promenade that would accommodate the most corseted and bustled of late Victorian ladies' style. In short, the threshold to the Iroquois provided a luxurious framework for patrons to display their fashionable frocks, reassuring visitors that they were in a respectable part of the city where safety could be expected.

Indeed, the Iroquois manager, Will J. Davis, took pains to promote the security of the theatre both to the general public and to the theatre artists booked to perform as part of the combination touring practice common to the time. On programs, letterhead, and newspaper advertisements, all references to the Iroquois were accompanied by the phrase "Absolutely Fireproof." While such claims were hardly unusual for the time, they nevertheless provide another clue about the gendered expectations for the audience (and performers) of the Iroquois: namely, that they needed masculine reassurance for their feminine fears. There was a kind of swaggering machismo behind the Syndicate's profit-driven rush to open the theatre before the holiday season, supported by the fact that it had been several years since a major theatre fire had broken out in the United States. Not one of the front-of-house staff members was trained to assist patrons in the event of a fire, for example. Even the house's much-publicized asbestos curtain was a cheap imitation of a fireproof one, containing no metal wiring for reinforcement and very little asbestos. The Syndicate's emphasis was on appearance and profit, not function or safety, as if any audience concerns about fire were silly and unfounded.

On the fateful day of the fire, December 30, thousands of patrons showed up for the Wednesday "bargain matinee" in hopes of seeing *Mr. Bluebeard*. Many of them were students and teachers on vacation, though the vast majority of the victims who would perish were housewives and children. As one of the actors on stage later recalled, "It struck me as I looked out over the crowd during the first act that I had never before seen so many women and children in the audience. Even the gallery was full of mothers and children. There were several parties of girls in their teens."[6] Although the house could officially seat 1,600, it was not uncommon to sell standing-room-only tickets to at least 100 extra spectators. On this cold and blustery afternoon, however, as many as 250 standing-room-only tickets were sold. So full was the house that the star of the show, Eddie Foy, had to provide his son a stool in the wings as there was no room in the house for him. Counting the performers and crew as well as the patrons, there were at least 2,300 people filling the Iroquois by 2 o'clock that afternoon.

The show they had crowded into the auditorium to see was a frothy extravaganza that Klaw and Erlanger had paid $150,000 to import from its successful run at Drury Lane in London. While most storybook versions of the Bluebeard tale centered around the cruelty of the title character who punished his wives for entering the forbidden chamber, since 1791 English audiences had enjoyed a lighter, melodramatic version of the myth that was later adapted into a pantomime. It was this "silly musical comedy" that the Syndicate exported to the United States.[7] Shortened for American attention spans (and altered to include blackface performance and references to Milwaukee beer), *Mr. Bluebeard* consisted of three acts played out in eleven scenes. The numerous costume and scenic changes (there were 1,600 costumes and 280 drops) strongly suggest that audiences were drawn to *Bluebeard* for the spectacle it promised rather than the story it told. That said, many patrons were familiar with the star,

Eddie Foy, who in 1890 had performed the title role in another variation on the Bluebeard theme (*Bluebeard Jr.,* a comic retelling in which the dead wives reanimate and ruthlessly torture their husband). In this British import, however, Foy played the role of Sister Anne, a relatively minor role that allowed for several comic bits in his bustle-laden costume. According to critics, the "girls" were the highlight of the production, especially the aerialist who flew on a trolley-wire out across the audience at the end of the second act.[8]

At approximately 3:15 in the afternoon, in the midst of the second act, the double-octet number "In the Pale Moonlight" began. All other lights on the stage were extinguished save "an eerie bluish tint" that came from a calcium arc light with a blue gel shining down from the iron bridge above the proscenium.[9] As was customary for the period, the wiring for this instrument was not bound by metal, so that it could remain flexible enough to be focused at will by its operator. Having directed the flood of light onto the stage, operator Patrick McNulty stepped away from his instrument momentarily; it was during his absence that the spark lit, flaring against the loose edges of a scenic drop. Not only was the drop made of fabric, it was covered in oil-based paint (as were all 280 drops, hung closely together). Within seconds, the flames began to spread.

Those who witnessed it backstage began to take action, trying desperately to beat the fire out of the fabric.[10] Remarkably, the performance continued without a hitch on stage for some time, thanks to the orchestra music drowning out the shouts from those backstage. Even when the fire spread visibly to the stage, the chorus continued to dance and sing, hoping to calm the audience and to avoid widespread panic. Their valiant efforts were fruitless, however: once spectators caught sight of the fire, they rose from their seats together as if they were parts of one body, and the terror spread through the house nearly as quickly as the drops caught fire.

At this point, I turn to the narrative of Mrs. Josephine Petry, a survivor of the fire, for an eyewitness account:

> It was the second act, the moonlight octette, if I am not mistaken, when I saw on the left hand side behind the proscenium arch a bright light. I kept my eyes on that, because to me it did not look right, and it got brighter all the time. Eddie Foy came right beside the proscenium arch, right where the fire was on the side, over him, and told the people they should keep their seats, there was no danger. Naturally a few got up, but they sat down again. Some people said "Keep your seats." I got up and some one said beside me: "Sit down, there is nothing the matter." I sat down again, but the glare was getting much brighter and pieces of charred cloth were falling down,

> although the flames by then had not come forward. They were all behind [the arch], but you could see the light so brightly I picked up my wraps and went out. . . . I went out by the same way I entered. At the lower floor about a hundred people were trying to get out. The doors were locked. When I left the charred remnants of the scenery were falling down in large chunks onto the stage, and the lights were so bright that they scared me, and I got up, but the flames had not reached the stage yet when I left, but when I got down to the exit and turned my head there was a mass of flames behind; it was all flames, and yet I did not hear a sound.[11]

As Petry's story demonstrates, several attempts were made by actors and fellow patrons to calm the audience, but ultimately the instinctive need to survive outweighed any desire to follow instruction. Upon their attempts to escape, however, most spectators had trouble finding the exits (in the push to open the theatre before the holiday season, Davis was encouraged by the Syndicate to postpone installing exit signage), and many of those who did locate an exit found the doors locked. For those lucky enough to have chosen an exit that wasn't locked, many were still unable to escape because the doors opened inward and the crush of the mob made them impossible to move. Perhaps the most egregious of the obstacles, however, was the fact that several of the balcony fire exits were never completed, leading many panicked spectators to make their only viable choice to escape the raging fire: they jumped out to the alley below. Although most of the earliest jumpers were killed upon impact, as the bodies began to pile up, others survived the fall. When it was all over, that alley became known as "Death Alley," and it was said that the deceased were piled ten bodies high.[12]

It was a gruesome scene, to be sure. What is striking about this tragedy, however, is the uncanny manner in which this event and its aftermath mirror the Bluebeard myth. In the story, the wife is locked out of the chamber of horrors (as, we assume, were all the wives before her), while in the Iroquois disaster the housewives (among other patrons) were locked *in*. Admittedly, this alone is a fairly tenuous link. However, when one considers the "lesson" taught by the Bluebeard legend, the parallels take on a deeper meaning.

In her 2004 book, *Secrets Beyond the Door: The Story of Bluebeard and His Wives*, Maria Tatar explores the pervasive nature of this tale in our cultural memory and its warnings against female epistemophilia (the desire to know). As she summarizes, "Bluebeard's wife is constructed as both agent of sexual betrayal and resourceful investigator," while "Bluebeard [himself] has come to be celebrated as a cultural hero."[13] In the aftermath of the Iroquois fire, Eddie Foy's heroism (for his attempts to calm the audience) was much celebrated, while the Syndicate was understandably vilified for its attention to profits over safety. Meanwhile, the female-dominated audience was characterized as both resourceful and hysterical.

There are other compelling comparisons to consider. For example, Bluebeard is typically cast as some kind of subaltern or "Other" ("oriental," generically foreign, or sometimes Jewish), while the wife is from Western Europe or the United Kingdom.[14] Mark Hodin notes how James S. Metcalfe caricatured the members of the Syndicate for their Jewish ethnicity during his tenure as drama editor at *Life* magazine; the viciousness with which he depicted them only grew stronger after the demise of the Iroquois.[15] The public's sympathy understandably lay with the victims of the fire, especially as the legal battles dragged on and ultimately justice eluded the victims' families.

While this is only a start at considering the connective thread between what was being shown on stage and the reactions taken by the matinee audience in peril, it is my hope that my discussion of this pivotal moment in theatre history will enrich our understanding not only of audience behavior but also of survivor narratives in general and their uncanny ability to mirror our folkloric understanding of how we (should) respond to danger.

Notes

1. Credit for my opening reference to Holmes goes to Arthur Martin, who reviewed Nat Brant's book *Chicago Death Trap* in 2003 (*Journal of the Illinois State Historical Society* 96, no. 2: 197–98) by referencing Holmes's remarks from his recorded opinion for the Court in *Schenck v. United States,* 294. The Iroquois Fire is cited as "the worst theater fire in U.S. history" in Lee Davis, *Man-Made Catastrophes* (New York: Checkmark Books, 2002), 235.

2. Dennis Kennedy, *The Spectator and the Spectacle: Audience in Modernity and Postmodernity* (Cambridge: Cambridge University Press, 2009), 3.

3. In considering the "threshold," I follow the lead of Susan Bennett's "On the threshold of theatre" (pp. 133–48) in the third chapter ("The Audience and Theatre") of her groundbreaking book *Theatre Audiences: A Theory of Production and Reception* (London: Routledge, 1990).

4. Perry R. Duis and Cathlyn Schallhorn, Introduction to *Chicago Death Trap: The Iroquois Fire of 1903* by Nat Brandt (Carbondale: Southern Illinois University Press, 2003), xiv.

5. Ibid., xv.

6. Eddie Foy, "A Tragedy Remembered," *NFPA Journal* (July–August 1995): 76.

7. Brandt, *Chicago Death Trap,* 18.

8. Ibid., 19.

9. Ibid., 30.

10. Ibid., 30–31.

11. Marshall Everett, *The Great Chicago Theater Disaster: The Complete Story Told By the Survivors* (Chicago: Publishers Union of America, 1904), 256.

12. See, for example, "Iroquois Theater Fire," *Weird Chicago.com*. 2006. Ed. Troy Taylor. *http://www.weirdchicago.com/iroquois.html* (accessed April 14, 2011).

13. Maria Tatar, *Secrets Beyond the Door: The Story of Bluebeard and His Wives* (Princeton, NJ: Princeton University Press, 2004), 172.

14. Ibid., chap. 1.

15. Mark Hodin, "The Disavowal of Ethnicity: Legitimate Theatre and the Social Construction of Literary Value in Turn-of-the-Century America," *Theatre Journal* 52, no. 2 (May 2000): 211–26.

Prosceniums and Screens

Audience Embodiment into the Digital Age

Becky Becker

IN *THE MAKING of American Audiences: From Stage to Television, 1750–1990,* Richard Butsch chronicles the history of audience development in the U.S. as it transitioned away from live theatre to film and television. According to Butsch, theatre owners in the early twentieth century "worried that people were leaving drama theater for the movies. The galleries were empty, they said, because the boys who had formerly sat there now frequented the movies."[1] Oh, how times do not change. But what is it about film that threatened to draw those early twentieth-century audiences away, well before the current conundrum of stadium seating, CGI, bigger and better 3D, and, perhaps even more aggravatingly convenient, streaming video? More fundamentally, what is it about the human brain, social conditioning, and human social interactions that have drawn such huge audiences to film since its inception? Is it merely the result of a more technologically focused society? Is it primarily the economics of film versus the economics of theatre? Or is it something to do with human embodiment and our conditioning over time?

Looking back on the critical moment of film's introduction to the spectrum of entertainments offered in American culture during the early 1900s, it would seem that class and convenience did play a large role in film's popularity over live theatre. As Butsch points out, "when people could not afford a theater or vaudeville ticket they could still muster a nickel for the movies. In the 1907–1908 recession many theaters closed but nickelodeons were booming. *Lippincott's* magazine said that the movies caused decreases in box office at legitimate and vaudeville theaters and disbanding of theater companies."[2]

Similarly, Robert Sklar asserts that movies "rose to the surface of cultural consciousness from the bottom up, receiving their principal support from the lowest and most invisible classes in American society."[3] Even when times were good, immigrant working-class audiences saved their nickels for the community store-front movie houses, while middle- and upper-class audiences came to enjoy the finely decorated, comfortable theatre houses bought or built for the moving picture shows.

In an ongoing effort to draw the middle class to the movies, producers incorporated strategies that tended to alienate working-class audiences. Producers publicized their efforts at reforming the cruder aspects of nickelodeon culture—disreputable content and the potential for lewd or rowdy conduct—in favor of family entertainment.[4] The change that seems to have had the greatest impact, however, was the movie theatre venue itself, as movie palaces of the 1910s and 1920s began to take the place of more community-oriented locales. In Butsch's estimation, "the essence of the picture palace was luxury at moderate prices, more expensive than the nickelodeon or the neighborhood house but less than big-time vaudeville or legitimate drama theaters. . . . It lured, then awed and silenced the audience. It shifted the predominant class of the movie house audience and changed the relationship of working-class patrons to the theater. While the middle class may have been attracted by the luxury they aspired to, working-class people felt out of place."[5] Essentially, the feature that drew upwardly mobile audiences into the movie palaces—plush surroundings and comfort—pushed working-class audiences away. Aside from affordability, the working-class attraction to movie theatres as "centers of communication and cultural diffusion" was trumped by the ideals of high culture and proper audience etiquette.[6]

Arguably, drama critics and producers of live theatre in the early twentieth century contributed to the situation with their laissez-faire attitude toward lowbrow theatrical forms such as melodrama. While their intent may have been to "strengthen" live theatre through selectivity, the result was quite the opposite, as Butsch remarks, "the growth of upscale movie theaters unnerved supporters of drama, who feared further loss of drama patrons to these luxury houses. Drama critics showed little concern for the cheap melodrama theaters closed by competition from nickelodeons; these had tainted the image of drama. With their demise, drama could more readily claim a place in high culture."[7] In essence, elitist critical values helped to bring about the demise of working-class entertainments under the purview of live theatre, just as the elitist venues of luxury movie palaces threatened to diminish audiences of live theatre more generally.

The Body and Silence

Sound systems entered the movie houses in the late 1920s and 1930s, effectively shushing audiences who became more interested in hearing the dialogue emanating from the screen than the dialogue surrounding them in the theatre. Like the "legitimate" theatres of the late nineteenth century, movie houses became venues of strict audience decorum and relatively passive spectatorship. Much like the posh theatres of the previous decade, the overall experience effectively "lured, then awed and silenced the audience," to reiterate Richard Butsch.[8]

However, cinema audiences have not remained silent. On the contrary, today's movie audiences can be found snacking on popcorn and soda, texting or tweeting friends about how lame or exciting their flick of choice is, talking back to the screen, or, in some venues, eating a burger and downing a beer. While silence may no longer be the barometer for proper audience decorum in the movie house, the experience is still based in the unique understanding of what it means to be embodied.

Succinctly describing the process of embodiment, Bruce McConachie notes in *Engaging Audiences* that "cognitive concepts arise, fundamentally, from the experience of the body in the world."[9] A basic cognitive concept is our understanding of the world through a front-back orientation, by which we experience the world around us and project a similar front-back bias. In other words, film screens and television screens have fronts and backs, in part, because the individuals who invented them experience the world from this perspective. Similarly, traditional proscenium theatres that comprised many of the early vaudeville, melodrama, and "legitimate" theatre houses of the early twentieth century, tend to reinforce a back-front perspective.

But what of it? If theatre houses and film houses both embrace a front-back orientation, then what does being embodied have to do with an individual's preference for film, TV, or other mediated experiences over live theatre? Certainly "liveness" in theatrical performance has been discussed at length in theatre and performance studies, and is, arguably, one of the differences between film and theatre that provides a unique draw, particularly for theatre audiences. While it may be true that live performance and mediatized performance are "rivals," to echo Philip Auslander, one form need not be canonized at the expense of the other.[10] However, the development and rapid implementation of television, home computers, the Internet, and social networks into our daily lives during the second half of the twentieth century has clearly conditioned audiences of both film and theatre in particular ways. Currently, economics and class play a role in audience preferences for film, just as in its early history. But it is our embodiment (paired with a dedicated, ongoing experience with back-front mediated forms of "liveness") that continues to bolster the film industry while drawing audiences away from live theatre.

Living in bodies that have fronts and backs naturally orients individuals to the world in particular ways. As George Lakoff and Mark Johnson describe in their book *Philosophy in the Flesh*, "We have faces and move in the direction we see. Our bodies define a set of fundamental orientations that we use not only in orienting ourselves, but in perceiving the relationship of one object to another."[11] Our perception of the world is linked to conceptual metaphors that aid in our understanding and engagement with people, objects, environments, and ideas. For example, our concept of "time" is based on an embodied metaphorical understanding of time as an entity that is both spatially conceived and capable of movement. Things happen in a certain space of time. Time passes. We perceive time to be in front of us and in back of us.[12] While time may seem to be a relatively simple concept, it is through conceptual metaphor—an embodied process—that our embodied selves are able to conceive of it.

As with the concept of time, we also project our front-back orientation onto things that do not readily adhere to our own embodied orientation.[13] For example, when referring to an object we might say, "The ball is behind that tree," assuming the tree has a "back" despite the tree's lack of front-back orientation. Similarly, the "house" or audience seating area in a typical proscenium theatre is usually perceived to possess a "front" and a "back," spurring such comments as "Project your voice to the back of the house." Interestingly, in this case, it is the actor who is facing the house, projecting to the "back" because this is the direction in which the perceived audience's backs would be facing. While the concept of front-back orientation is mostly unconscious due to our embodied experience in the world, it has a rather profound impact on our perceptions and interactions.

The Body and Liveness

The fact of embodiment, paired with conventional forms of entertainment (film, television, and computer-related diversions), provides comfortable, predictable, and relatively passive interaction. Particularly with film and television, there are no decisions to be made other than which program or movie to see. The camera provides only a limited range of visceral content for the viewer to process, so the spectator need not choose where to look. If a spectator, interacting with this controlled vision, should happen to cry out, talk to a friend nearby, or otherwise make noise, the film will not be impacted (even if the other audience members are). There is an ease with which viewers approach the content because it is both controlled and comfortable, catering not only to their front-back embodied state but also to their experiences with mediated forms of liveness over time. While a "live" studio audience might serve to "trouble" the perspective of viewers of television due to the audience's invisibility in the finished product, its place in the overall image does not require a range of choices but reinforces the camera's exclusive vision. The movie screen, television screen, computer screen, and, more recently, the cell phone and digital notebook screen are all "containers" of the real or imagined action. Our relationship to these containers of action is defined through our embodiment. In an earlier work, *Metaphors We Live By,* Lakoff and Johnson persuasively describe this state of being: "We are physical beings, bounded and set off from the rest of the world by the surface of our skins, and we experience the rest of the world as outside us. Each of us is a container, with a bounding surface and an in-out orientation. We project our own in-out orientation onto other physical objects that are bounded by surfaces. Thus we also view them as containers with an inside and an outside."[14] Similarly, because we perceive ourselves to be "contained" within a body, we use this embodied concept to explain other states of being. If we are upset or off-balance emotionally, we might say we are "beside ourselves"; when someone responds in a way that we perceive to be illogical or uncontrolled we might say they are "out to lunch." On a more positive note, when we seek to empathize with others, we might say we want to "get out of ourselves," or "move out of our comfort zone," implying that there are moments when being "contained" is less desirable. Through metaphorical language, we reflect our own embodied understanding of what containment means.[15]

Just as our embodied experience encourages us to understand ourselves and objects in the world around us as "containers," we relate with greater ease to forms of entertainment that are similarly "contained." When we interact with a movie, a television program, or YouTube video, the exchange is controlled because there is no danger that the "container" outside ourselves will respond. Even when interacting via social networking, our "performance" is controlled due to our ability to effectively edit ourselves. (The recent suicide of a young gay man whose sexual experience was broadcast "live" via Facebook is just one example of the potential dangers of social network performances.)[16] Despite an arguably false sense of control, our embodied experience of increasingly sophisticated and "interactive" forms of technology may actually serve to amplify our desire for the comfort of "containment."

The Body and Desire

In her book *Theatre Audiences,* Susan Bennett notes that for many film theorists "the real signifiers of theatre performance restrict the imaginative involvement of the audience with the stage world."[17] In other words, live performers and the reality of the world before them prevent the audience from engaging fully on an abstract, imaginative level. Yet, human embodiment and our physical understanding of the world around us dispute this notion. If our knowledge of the world is based on metaphorical representations of concrete experiences, as cognitive science reveals, it follows that embodied individuals engage more readily on an abstract level to live theatrical experience.

Does the comfort of continuous front-back bodily engagement go directly against the desires of an embodied being? Is audience "comfort" the reason that theatre audiences have moved en masse toward film, television, and the increasingly popular streaming video that can be watched whenever the "audience" chooses? As Americans become more connected to technology that creates a static physical relationship with the world, will they inevitably desire more active, visceral entertainment that takes them on a physical journey rather than a digital and voyeuristic one?

My instincts about what it means to live in a body tell me "yes." Unmediatized liveness fuels audience desire: spectators make choices about what to look at. Actors, stage managers, and technicians make in-the-moment choices that interact with, and impact, audience choices. Susan Bennett asserts that "the theatre audience shares with the spectator of an art work the inability to take in everything with a single look, but, where the art work remains for subsequent looks, the theatrical performance is ephemeral. Pleasure results precisely from the ephemerality, from the necessity of making a selection of the elements offered."[18] The living, breathing moment, here and gone in an instant, remains one of the most powerful aspects of live performance. Perhaps more poignantly, it suits bodily experience and its desires since our front-back orientation in the world also produces a kind of "embodied ephemerality." Most of us experience the world in bodies with fronts accompanied by vision that provides our primary view of the world. Yet, we are also embodied with backs that do not allow literal vision but other sensual and physical perceptions. Just as there are limits to the theatrical experience, there are limits to our embodied experience of the world. Ephemerality is an embodied concept, connected to desire and based in our physical experience in the world. Again, to quote Bennett, "The spectator cannot experience pleasure without experiencing its limits."[19] We sit facing a table, eyes focused on our reading, yet we feel eyes on us from behind. We hear the sound of a familiar voice approaching from behind and perceive its warmth without being able to see. We desire to know what we cannot know and seize the moment even as it slips from our grasp. One of the ways that theatre spectators experience the pleasure of the ephemeral is through choices made in looking and perceiving as well as in the embodied sense of the moment that slips away.

If "embodied ephemerality" is a concept useful to human experience, and more specifically to theatre practitioners, what then? What kinds of theatre experiences provide engagement that defies the comfortable, the predictable, the contained? Among many examples are performance art that privileges spectator interaction; groups like the Neo-Futurists of Chicago and No Shame Theatre in Columbus, Georgia; "devised" works developed and performed across the country. I document such an experience in a personal journal created after seeing a performance by Shunt, a London-based company, on June 24, 2005, in their space below the London Bridge Tube Station:

> Tonight I had the most sensational experience. I feel as if I don't need to see anything else. . . . *Tropicana* at the Shunt Vaults—how do I begin? . . . There was a que [*sic*], but after a brief wait we were allowed into an odd space filled w/cleaning chemicals, etc. Then an odd man sort of directed us to go through a locker into another space lined with doors on the walls, small cubbyhole "bars" for purchasing beer or wine, and doors w/peepholes through which we could peer. . . . It was already unnerving to be in the space that was slowly filling with people. The air was musty and it became quite warm. Images through the peepholes . . . a puppy, two towers collapsing (not the Twin Towers, but like that), a woman looking back . . . a man standing in a corridor in a white coat. . . . Eventually, we were escorted into an elevator shaft by a man in a uniform who was later designated as the "hero," I think. We "traveled" on the elevator and when the doors opened two girls in nightclub attire (feather headdresses and bikinis) popped at us from the dark, then we were plunged into darkness and had to grope along to the next room. There, we were given glimpses of the woman from the peephole in a lab coat, climbing on what turned out to be cages. She spoke of the animals who had all gone, of having sex and talking shop, but wanting to make love, of holding a bunny too tightly. A man joined her. She told us to open an envelope she left behind if she wasn't back in a couple of minutes. The "hero" appeared on video to instruct us to our next venue. He spoke through a dummy dressed like him—in an elevator man's uniform. . . . We moved to the next space after I and a man near the front opened the envelope. Inside was a Kellwood Mint Cake, I think it was called. I told him to give it to his girlfriend. As we moved to our destination—left, left and right toward the blue light—we passed a sort

of greenhouse, dimly lit, with someone inside. . . . When we got to the next space, it was sort of open and vaulted with "low walls" on which we could sit—benches, really, in a way.[20]

And now the journal goes into fragments, a frenetic attempt to pour the images in my head onto the page as quickly and vividly as possible:

Sensory explosion. Darkness. Sounds of trains. Nervous laughter. Spasms of light. Woman coming out of locker. Woman smashing pineapple on the ground—man doing the same further off. Sounds of discomfort from audience members. Hairs prickling all over me. Tropicana girls dancing in pools of light. Man in elevator moving sideways through corridor. Woman moving upside down suspended through corridor. . . . First aid car moving back up tunnel from where we came. Weeping. Shirtless guitar player leading black-clad Tropicana girls—chained to car and pulling it while weeping—back up the tunnel. This time it's a hearse with flowers & body inside. We follow. At the other end of the tunnel there is a wake. Black-clad Tropicana girls dance & do aerial stunts with car. Box office woman sells beer when dance is over. We are told the boy/man/hero has died. War is mentioned. The autopsy will begin in ten minutes.[21]

An autopsy did ensue ten minutes later, but like none I could have ever imagined. One last journal line sums up the conclusion of the performance: "Artaud would be thrilled."[22]

This was an incredibly visceral theatre experience—though not necessarily one that all audiences would enjoy. I am not suggesting this kind of performance as the sole solution to engaging audiences and accessing their sense of "embodied ephemerality." Still, it effectively drew me out of the front-back audience mode with which I am so accustomed. It drew me out of my "container" mentality, out of my acquaintance with comfort, and into a more fully realized engagement of my entire body, all my senses: an "embodied ephemerality" that makes live theatre so very worth the journey.

Notes

1. Richard Butsch, *The Making of American Audiences: From Stage to Television, 1750–1990* (Cambridge: Cambridge University Press, 2000), 150.
2. Ibid.
3. Robert Sklar, *Movie-Made America: A Cultural History of American Movies* (New York: Vintage, 1994), 3.
4. Butsch, *The Making of American Audiences*, 154–61.
5. Ibid., 161.
6. Sklar, *Movie-Made America*, 18.

7. Butsch, *The Making of American Audiences,* 162.

8. Ibid., 161.

9. Bruce McConachie, *Engaging Audiences* (New York: Palgrave Macmillan, 2008), 39.

10. Philip Auslander, *Liveness: Performance in a Mediatized Culture* (New York: Routledge, 1999), 1.

11. George Lakoff and Mark Johnson, *Philosophy in the Flesh: The Embodied Mind and Its Challenge to Western Thought* (New York: Basic Books, 1999), 34.

12. Ibid., 137–69.

13. For a more nuanced discussion of time, as well as exceptions to the front-back orientation of time, see Lakoff and Johnson, *Philosophy in the Flesh,* 139–41.

14. George Lakoff and Mark Johnson, *Metaphors We Live By* (Chicago: University of Chicago Press, 1980), 29.

15. For a more detailed discussion of "Self as Container," see Lakoff and Johnson's *Philosophy in the Flesh,* 274–77.

16. For a more detailed account of this incident: Lisa W. Foderaro, "Private Moment Made Public, Then a Fatal Jump," *New York Times* (September 29, 2010). http://www.nytimes.com/2010/09/30/nyregion/30suicide.html (Retrieved September 3, 2011).

17. Susan Bennett, *Theatre Audiences* (New York: Routledge, 1997), 15.

18. Ibid., 73.

19. Ibid.

20. Becky Becker, Unpublished Journal (London, England: Summer 2005).

21. Ibid.

22. Ibid.

Annie Oakley and the Disruption of Victorian Expectations

Lisa Bernd

THIS ONGOING project to consider the legacy of Annie Oakley's performances began when I came upon a framed poster of Buffalo Bill's Wild West in the lobby of the Western History Collection at the University of Oklahoma. I was surprised when the images made me recall my own childhood in suburbia. Despite the fact that I grew up on Long Island during the 1970s, I had played cowboys and Indians, always insisting on impersonating Annie Oakley. This play scenario was perhaps the closest I came to being treated as an equal among the neighborhood boys. Letting me play with their cap pistols and ride my invisible horse next to theirs, they allowed me to be the hero—after I had finished cleaning up the cabin, of course.[1] Ironically, by framing my play within gender expectations that included domestic chores, I was able to experience what performance theorist Peta Tait labels "moments of freedom" from those expectations—moments where I was able to run with the boys and capture (or even be) the "bad guy."[2]

As a female sharpshooter, Annie Oakley traveled the world precisely because she could do a "man's work" while appearing to adhere to the conventions of Victorian femininity. By framing her own "moments of freedom" in gendered gesture and behavior, Oakley was fundamental to the construction of a modern "American" identity for women. Modeling authority and self-sufficiency, as well as a spiffy pair of pantaloons, Annie Oakley influenced American women while fostering the national enterprise of cultural unification. Theorizing that "the Wild West" was an effort toward the creation of a national identity, I consider the way Annie Oakley's presence cultivated an American identity for women by embodying freedoms typically denied to women in the Victorian era.

Although Oakley refused to align herself politically with the feminist movement, her dress, actions, and associations resulted from the freedom she experienced as a performer, especially as a woman doing "man's" work. That her audience came to accept and idolize her speaks volumes about her ability to disrupt audience expectations to accommodate social change.

If, as Benedict Anderson suggests, nations are "imagined communities," then it was particularly important, at the end of the nineteenth century, for the United States to establish itself firmly in the imaginations of its own inhabitants as well as Europeans. Buffalo Bill's theatrical representation of frontier life offered an alternative to the prevalent European ethno-linguistic model of nationalism.[3] The late nineteenth century proved a highly volatile period of European nationalism as groups constantly tried to partition territory according to historical ethnic demographics. Without ethnicity or history in common, cultural diversity and regional divisions were seen as the U.S.'s biggest threat to a cohesive nation. Clearly, however, the violent and oppressive dynamic of colonialism implicit in the "taming" of the frontier demonstrates that, for the United States, nationalism was not a matter of political self-determination but, ironically and inescapably, one of cultural recognition in a world where homogeneous ethnicity was "the decisive or even the only criteria of potential nationhood."[4] No wonder, then, that international cultural expositions of all kinds flourished during this period. In the United States, a site of multicultural and multiethnic inevitability, those expositions often took the form of "Wild West" shows that deliberately capitalized on the exotic composition of its diversity.

Buffalo Bill Cody ran the largest and most popular Wild West show. His show included a cast and crew of over 600 as well as 400 horses. At one point, the show played 131 locations in 190 days. Incongruously, despite his own participation in the destruction of Native American culture, Buffalo Bill's show supported the idea that cultural diversity contributed to the strength of the nation. Roger Hall, in *Performing the American Frontier: 1870–1906*, argues that by framing the appearance/participation of Native Americans within a context of education and "cultural" enrichment and highlighting the contributions of diverse peoples in the "Rough Riders of the World" act, Buffalo Bill defended the United States's multicultural existence while other struggling nations clearly rejected ideas of "inclusion."[5] Between 1882 and 1913, the millions of people who saw his show in a dozen countries were exposed to a version of the white settlement of the West that claimed to be genuine. While many of the performers in the show had actually participated in the Western movement, the reenactments were melodramatic and spectacularly distorted. Cody romanticized the brutal, bloody, and fatal colonization of the West "until the truth was so totally mixed with the myth as to be indistinguishable."[6]

It is not surprising that this blurring of narrative boundaries spilled over into the biography of Cody's biggest star, Annie Oakley. To a large degree, creative marketing shaped Oakley's foundational myth as a symbol of the best the West had to offer and, to this day, popular biographies of Annie Oakley continue to tell the story everyone knows. Born and raised hundreds of miles from the frontier, Phoebe Ann Moses of Darke County, Ohio, learned to shoot as the result of abject poverty. Hagiography insists that, while watching her widowed mother and six siblings go hungry in the two-room cabin they occupied, "Annie," as she was known, took her dead father's rifle off the mantle to try her hand at hunting. When her very first shot successfully provided the family with a rabbit dinner, her mother encouraged her to continue honing her hunting skills. Later, at the age of fifteen, Annie competed against the already-successful gun performer Frank Butler in a local sharpshooting contest and beat him. Familiar interpretations would have it that Oakley's career was born that instant, but her act did not develop until after their marriage and a disruption in Butler's employment.[7]

Recent biographies continue to treat Oakley as a singular phenomenon, virtually unconnected to social and cultural discourse. In her article "Annie Oakley and Her Ideal Husband of No Importance," Tracy C. Davis suggests that biographies of Oakley have been traditionally structured "in the manner of romance narratives . . . retaining the typical emphasis on successive victorious turns with adversity."[8] Davis goes on to argue that treating Oakley's biography as "romance narrative" hides the material ways in which Oakley destabilized the ideals of Victorian "womanhood." Biographer Glenda Riley acknowledges Oakley's contributions to feminism in her book *The Life and Legacy of Annie Oakley,* but even Riley is reluctant to concede Oakley's difficult negotiations with the dominant culture in both her performances and personal life. Riley seems to view the contradiction between Oakley's athletic achievement, her performance choices, and her lifestyle as socially constructed but "naturally" accepted by Oakley. Riley writes: "For years, Annie had ranked ladylike conduct high on her list of priorities. Both her Quaker background and her Midwestern values encouraged her to accept many of the era's prescriptions regarding true womanhood." Documented incidents where Oakley reveals her "tough, sarcastic, and even disrespectful side" are glossed over as minor personality "flaws," although Riley reports that she seemed proud of her independent attitudes.[9]

In shying away from a critical understanding of Oakley's contribution to both the national enterprise of cultural unification and her influence on American women, popular biographers pay little attention to how, consciously or unconsciously, Oakley contributed to the development of the feminist movement and improved the status of women. Like any theatrical representation, Annie Oakley's work both supported and transformed popular ideology. Bill Dunstone, in his article "Performing Colonial Bodies and (as) Work," asserts, "theatre representation must, as representation, displace and transform the dominant to some degree, rather than simply replicate it."[10] Oakley's displacement of gender expectations turned out to be fundamental to the construction of an "American" identity, an identity that continues to influence the country's political, social, and economic development as women continue to fight for equal rights. As my twenty-first-century encounters with the poster images illustrate, Annie Oakley continues to attract an audience. This longevity, along with the extraordinary cultural significance of her performances, makes evaluating her impact especially challenging.

Clearly, Oakley's audience of the 1970s (my youth) saw her as an adventurer: a brave, strong, energetic woman who was admired and emulated. In her own day, Annie Oakley was one of the most famous women in the world and topped a "worldwide circulation of performers" that included Jenny Lind, Sarah Bernhardt, Henry Irving, Mark Twain, and Charles Dickens. She performed before audiences not only in the United States but in France, Austria, Germany, Holland, England, Spain, Russia, and Italy (including Sardinia, Corsica, Venice, and The Vatican), among others. Her audiences famously included the Prince of Wales, Queen Victoria, Kaiser Wilhelm, the Grand Duke of Russia, and, reportedly, Czar Alexander II.[11]

Queen Victoria is, perhaps, her most famous fan. That she was so popular with the conservative queen is especially surprising since Oakley embodied the tension between Victorian mores and modern progress for women. While most historians are quick to point out Oakley's modest dress, love of flowers, and penchant for tea as evidence of her Victorian values, the foundation of her career and personal life was the very opposite of corseted Victorian femininity.

Despite her popularity abroad, Oakley's central and perhaps crucial audience was, and remains, Americans. As my childhood memories suggest, the history of the West and its images play a large part in forming our communal identity. "The image that Americans have of themselves," writes Sarah Blackstone in *Buckskins, Bullets, and Business: A History of Buffalo Bill's Wild West,* "and the image that Europeans have of Americans is closely tied to both the reality and the myth of the American West."[12] Because Wild West shows were most popular in the eastern United

States and Europe, they symbolically represented the character of the newly colonized western region. This became particularly important as the United States struggled to develop a cohesive identity among a diverse population that was continually growing from waves of immigration. Wild West shows provided an opportunity for this region to show the rest of the country their "victory" in "subduing the wilderness" and thus their contribution to the manifest destiny of the nation.[13]

But the Wild West also provided an opportunity for women that may, over time, have been far more significant in the development of the nation. In this popular, public venue, women were afforded the opportunity to experience a measure of equality. An acknowledged advocate of women's rights, Cody was known to offer women equal pay: "One of the few places of equal pay for equal work: What we want to do is give our women even more liberty than they have. Let them do any kind of work that they see fit, and if they do it as well as men, give them the same pay."[14]

It is unlikely that these messages about equality were lost on the audience. In fact, a proclamation such as this seems tailor-made for marketing—an invitation to the audience to evaluate the accomplishments of the female performers. Cody, a very successful entrepreneur, knew the demographics of his audience. While it is hard to imagine that the violence, dirt, and mayhem of the Wild West would have been attractive to Victorian women, the show was clearly marketed to families. Advertising frequently highlighted affordability and convenient transportation.

Moreover, women were now the core audience at theatrical matinees and exhibition entertainments. Richard Butsch, in *The Making of American Audiences: From Stage to Television, 1750–1990,* documents the "regendering" of the theatre in the mid-nineteenth century when the theatre was redefined as a place for women and children, particularly at matinees. The female audience grew until the turn of the century when a backlash against "matinee girls" created a "high culture/low culture" divide.[15] Cody countered that divide by appealing to a broad spectrum of spectators through the representation of patriotism, exoticism, heroism, and a carefully framed egalitarianism.

In fact, Buffalo Bill counted on Annie Oakley to embody these meticulously selected qualities by showcasing her femininity to support the violence and authenticity of the show. In *Buffalo Bill's Wild West: Celebrity, Memory, and Popular History,* Joy S. Kasson writes: "[by 1893] Annie Oakley's shooting act was now firmly placed at the beginning of the show, for experience had proved that audiences who felt nervous when confronted with the noise and smoke of gunfire felt reassured when they saw a petite, attractive woman shooting first."[16]

Performance theorist Peta Tait describes the kind of freedom from the limitations of gender identity Oakley must have experienced when she explains the work of female trapeze artists. In her article, "Disappearing the Feminine in Aerial Performance," Tait describes these performances as moments of release from the physical constraints of gender—the precise instant of "flying" serving as the escape hatch. The trapeze artist's feminine body, maintains Tait, "is overtaken by the physical body moving through space." At the same time, she explains, the trapeze artist's performance depends on, and encourages, the audience's assumptions about the female body in order to enhance the spectator's "appreciation" of the performance. The entire performance, then, is framed, before and after the actual "flying" by deliberate signs of gender: hips thrust forward, backs arched, heads tossed, arms thrown into the "TA-DA!" stance.[17] Similarly, signs of femininity that deemed her participation in gunplay nonthreatening framed Annie Oakley's performances. Like Tait's aerialists, Oakley structured her act within a context of femininity in order to escape the physical limitations of gender and to make their achievements in traditionally male activities more palatable and more appreciated.

Oakley supported her performance with physical gestures that were consistent with her image. Her entrance usually took the form of a light running step followed by a small curtsey. She often deliberately tripped over her own feet during a run of shots as a way to make the trick look harder than it was. This, in combination with the kisses she blew and the way she exited with a little kick, made her all the more endearing to the public and the press. Interestingly, not one account that I have come across in my research suggests that this coyness was a genuine part of Oakley's personality. Rather, contemporary writers such as Davis and Riley credit her with great acting ability, a sense of spectacle, and a blatant desire to be popular. This motif of "feminine incompetence," among other theatrical elements, guided the audience to read Oakley's act in positive relation to the status quo.

By coding her act in a specifically gendered fashion, Oakley managed not to offend contemporary social and gender sensibilities. This strategy still works today. Racecar driver Danica Patrick and snowboarder Gretchen Bleiler are but two examples of female athletes who have gained popularity by embodying accepted ideas about women and femininity—usually in advertising and *Playboy.* While Oakley and these women transgress social norms by participating in traditionally male-dominated athletic events, they simultaneously reinforce gender conventions by "contraven[ing] the separation of masculine and feminine behaviors while maintaining the display of gender identity."[18]

Newspaper accounts report Oakley's strengths to have been speed and agility. (She was also ambidextrous, a rare skill for a sharpshooter: with a pistol in each hand, she could accurately fire both guns simultaneously.) Reporters frequently commented on her confidence and athleticism. This athletic ability was perhaps most clearly demonstrated in one of her most popular stunts: "[Oakley] laid a shotgun in the dirt about 10 feet on the far side of her gun table. She hurried back around to the other side of the table and waited for Butler to spring a clay pigeon. As he released it, she ran forward, leaped over the table, picked up her shotgun and broke the bird before it landed. This was an astonishing routine since it took only 4 or 5 seconds from the time the bird was released for it to hit the ground."[19] Those few seconds represent a freedom of movement that must have been nothing less than exhilarating for both Oakley and the spectators. For women, her act represented not only the physical freedom demonstrated in the stunt, but the freedom to travel, pursue a career and, perhaps most important, the freedom from restrictive Victorian dress. There was, after all, little chance that Oakley could hurdle the table in a corset and petticoats.

As in the case of Tait's circus flyers, these freedoms needed to be framed within socially recognized norms. While her petite stature made her athletic abilities seem all the more remarkable to the press, Oakley capitalized on Victorian social values by seeming to dress quite modestly. She sewed her own pearl-buttoned leggings to be worn under short skirts. This ensured that her legs did not show while allowing the necessary freedom of movement. These iconic outfits now appear to seamlessly enrobe our epistemology of Oakley. Biographers view her wardrobe as evidence that Oakley clung, within the limits of practicality, to Victorian principles of dress. In fact, one of her most famous and photographed costumes is strikingly similar to an outfit (fringed coat and fringed leggings) that Buffalo Bill wore in *The Scouts of the Prairie*.[20] This sartorial blurring of feminine and masculine was still deeply troubling to American civilian society.[21] In addition to flying under the radar of the audience's expectation of dress, Oakley did something much more remarkable. Despite her protestations, she aligned herself, deliberately or not, with the failed dress reform movement of Amelia Bloomer.

The dress reform movement—an effort to change women's wardrobes from tight corsets and heavy, overly full skirts—was first advocated by utopian religious groups such as the Oneida Community and feminists such as Elizabeth Cady Stanton and Amelia Bloomer (for whom the telltale garment of a dress-reformer is named). But, by 1879, the movement had largely died out; women were as confined as ever by their garments. Bloomer herself had put up with so much ridicule she acquiesced and accepted the "crinoline" as sufficient reform. Even ranching and rodeo women, such as Lucille Mulhall, could make no progress in changing social expectations of dress despite the number of debilitating and even fatal injuries suffered by these women.[22] How, then, did audiences come to accept Oakley's outfits—shockingly similar in silhouette and function to those endorsed by early feminists? When Oakley's archrival and fellow Wild West performer Lillian Smith was criticized in the press for dressing too "manly," her popularity immediately began to slip, much to Oakley's delight.[23] (In fact, it is almost impossible to distinguish the real differences in dress between the two performers.) Apparently, "mannish" activities were fine, as long as they weren't performed in "mannish" costumes.

The dress reform movement advocated shorter skirts and pantaloons instead of long skirts with restrictive supportive garments such as corsets. One concern among reformers was for reproductive health. The failure to explain reproductive disease meant that fashionable dress was a logical suspect for disorders unique to women.[24] Annie Oakley had no children and Tracy Davis suggests that her early years with Frank Butler, before she joined the act, may have been spent trying to become pregnant.[25] If that is true, dress reform would have caught her attention as surely as assisted reproductive technologies have captured the attention of women today.

Oakley's wardrobe and its connection to dress reform was, in fact, a topic of discussion among spectators and the press. Reportedly, Oakley found it necessary to respond negatively: "I don't like bloomers or bloomer women, but I think that sport and healthful exercise make women better, healthier, and happier."[26] I'm reminded here of Ibsen's similar disavowal of feminism when he was asked about *Doll's House.* Whatever Oakley and subsequent biographers may have thought, there is no question that the silhouette she created was remarkably similar to the bloomers costume. In addition, the agendas for both Oakley and the movement were identical. Like the dress reform movement, Oakley made the connection between health and fashion. She understood that dress was essential to her profession and proved it by creating her own costumes. Wearing long, heavy skirts and corsets meant that muscles were used differently. Athletic ability depended on a different style of dress. Additionally, mental illness was connected to women's dress. Changing too frequently was thought to render a woman mentally unstable. A love of fashion was thought of as an illness. Fashionable women were "fragile"; that was an association Oakley could not afford. She understood that strength and vitality were important aspects of her image.

Perhaps audiences overlooked Oakley's gender transgressions because she did not identify herself as a feminist or a suffragette. But not all dress reformers were suffragettes. In fact, they saw themselves as individuals apart from mass social movements (such as feminism) and feared what fashionable women might do with the vote.[27] According to biographer Shirl Kasper, Oakley held the same opinion.[28]

Amy Kesselman, in her article "The 'Freedom Suit': Feminism and Dress Reform in the United States, 1848–1975," writes that dress reform "represents a different brand of feminism from that of the women's rights movement" and a "road not taken" by nineteenth-century feminism.[29] Dress reformers were committed to an "exemplary action" model of social change which assumed that a few intrepid individuals with the courage to live according to principle could inspire enough other people to transform the world.[30]

There is no question that Annie Oakley's performances did, and continue to, "transform the world." In my childhood world, I was free to run with the boys and never miss a shot—because of Annie Oakley. As in the case of Tait's circus flyers, Oakley showed American women how to stretch social and cultural boundaries and found "moments of freedom" in movement and dress by framing truly transgressive acts within socially recognized norms. While audiences may have interpreted Oakley's athleticism and dress as nonthreatening, it was perhaps only because the lens they were looking through was inscribed with kisses and curtseys.

Notes

1. My experience is certainly not unique. See Ann McGrath, "Playing Colonial: Cowgirls, Cowboys, and Indians in Australia and North America," *Journal of Colonialism and Colonial History* 2, no. 1 (2001). McGrath writes about playing cowboys and Indians in her native Australia as a kind of transnational phenomenon.

2. Peta Tait, "Feminine Free Fall: A Fantasy of Freedom," *Theatre Journal* 48, no. 1 (March 1, 1996): 27–34.

3. Benedict Anderson, *Imagined Communities: Reflections on the Origin and Spread of Nationalism* (New York: Verso, 1991).

4. E. J. Hobsbawm, *Nations and Nationalism since 1780: Programme, Myth, Reality* (Cambridge: Canto, 1992), 64, 102.

5. For an extended discussion of the relationship between ethnicity, Wild West performance, and the idea of manifest destiny, see Roger Hall, *Performing the American Frontier: 1870–1906* (Cambridge: Cambridge University Press, 2001).

6. Sarah J. Blackstone, *Buckskins, Bullets, and Business: A History of Buffalo Bill's Wild West* (New York: Greenwood, 1986), 1.

7. Oakley and Butler married on August 23, 1876. They first performed together May 1, 1882.

8. Tracy C. Davis, "Annie Oakley and Her Ideal Husband of No Importance," *Critical Theory and Performance,* ed. Joseph Roach and Janelle Reinelt (Ann Arbor: University of Michigan Press, 1992), 299–300.

9. Glenda Riley, *The Life and Legacy of Annie Oakley* (Norman: University of Oklahoma Press, 1994), 112.

10. Bill Dunstone, "Performing Colonial Bodies and (as) Work," *Body Show/s: Australian Viewings of Live Performance,* ed. Peta Tait (Atlanta: Rodopi, 2000), 29–43.

11. Joy S. Kasson, *Buffalo Bill's Wild West: Celebrity, Memory, and Popular History* (New York: Hill and Wang, 2000), 66.

12. Blackstone, *Buckskins,* 1.

13. Ibid.

14. Chris Enss, *Buffalo Gals: Women of Buffalo Bill's Wild West* (Guilford: Globe Pequot, 2006).

15. Richard Butsch, *The Making of American Audiences: From Stage to Television, 1750–1990* (Cambridge: Cambridge University Press, 2000), 67, 121–26.

16. Kasson, *Buffalo Bill's Wild West,* 112.

17. Peta Tait, "Disappearing the Feminine in Aerial Performance," *Women and Performance* 7, no. 1 (self-published, 1993), 82.

18. Tait, "Feminine Free Fall," 27.

19. Shirl Kasper, *Annie Oakley* (Norman: University of Oklahoma Press, 1992), 43.

20. Kasson, *Buffalo Bill's Wild West,* 40.

21. Catherine Smith and Cynthia Greig, *Women in Pants: Manly Maidens, Cowgirls, and Other Renegades* (New York: Abrams, 2003), 12–18.

22. Mary Lou LeCompte, *Cowgirls of the Rodeo: Pioneer Professional Athletes* (Urbana: University of Illinois Press, 1993), 34–35.

23. Kasper, *Annie Oakley,* 87. See also *London Evening News,* July 19, 1887.

24. Gayle V. Fischer, *Pantaloons and Power: A Nineteenth-Century Dress Reform in the United States* (Kent, Ohio: Kent State University Press, 2001), 25.

25. Davis, "Annie Oakley and Her Ideal Husband," 302.

26. Smith and Greig, *Women in Pants,* 75.

27. Amy Kesselman, "The 'Freedom Suit': Feminism and Dress Reform in the United States, 1848–1975," *Gender and Society* 5, no. 4 (December 1991), 495–510.

28. Kasper, *Annie Oakley,* 213.

29. Kesselman, "The 'Freedom Suit,'" 495.

30. Ibid.

Thomas King at Sadler's Wells and Drury Lane

How the Audience (Mis)Read Management

Evan Bridenstine

FROM THE time David Garrick became co-proprietor and acting manager of Drury Lane in the 1747–1748 season to his retirement at the end of the 1775–1776 season, management at Drury Lane came to mean the presence of Garrick—both on and off the stage. Within that span of time, both Samuel Foote and George Colman had embodied a similar model at the Haymarket. However, the theatrical public had dealt directly with Garrick, and, thus, directly with management, for almost thirty years. Scholars writing on Garrick's career have noted the distinctive status granted to him by this long tenure. For example, in "David Garrick, Manager: Notes on the Theatre as a Cultural Institution in England in the Eighteenth Century," Dougald MacMillan describes Garrick's leading role within the management as that of "a public official": MacMillan credits Garrick's social position, his personal popularity as an actor, his frugality, and his "manager's sense" for his success in leading Drury Lane.[1] With his portrayal of Garrick as the guardian of a social institution, MacMillan also assumes that the public equated Drury Lane with David Garrick, an equation referred to in the remainder of this paper as the "Garrick blend."

After Garrick's retirement, the model of active, visible management linked with ownership shifted to one of passive, perhaps even indifferent ownership separated from management under Richard Brinsley Sheridan, evidenced best by the swift succession of managers, including Sheridan himself, Thomas Sheridan (his father), Joseph Younger (a former manager of Covent Garden), Thomas King (leading comedian at Drury Lane after Garrick's retirement), and Thomas Linley Sr. (Sheridan's father-in-law). Having filled the post of manager for the 1782–1783 season and then touring during the 1783–1784 season, King resumed the management the following year (1784–1785) and kept it until his swift resignation in September 1788 prepared the way for John Philip Kemble to assume authority. As can be seen in this brief summary, Drury Lane passed through a period of shifting identity without restoring the Garrick blend with a new management "face"; although members of Sheridan's family provided management for most of the seasons between Garrick and Kemble, only King's sustained (though relatively brief) tenure recreated anything similar to the Garrick blend.

King's managerial career ended with his position at Drury Lane, but his tenure there should be considered a final entry rather than an unusual event. King had served as part of the management of several theatres earlier in his career, and he had managed Sadler's Wells for just over a decade immediately prior to Drury Lane. To some extent, King had provided the entering management at Wells with its own "Garrick" blend, addressing the public both in the press and from the stage, so his selection as acting manager for Drury Lane allowed the public to reassert rather than redefine the blend. In fact, King's presence at the Wells had redefined management there.

By the time King purchased a controlling share in Sadler's Wells in 1772, that summer venue had come to be known for tumbling and rope dancing, but its offerings also included two major pantomimes each year. Direct competition for the Wells came in various forms: regular drama at the Haymarket and, for the initial and closing weeks of the summer season, Drury Lane and Covent Garden; public concerts at music gardens such as the Pantheon; masquerades held at private residences or hired halls; equestrian performances at Astley's Amphitheatre or Hughes's Riding School; displays of portraits or other novelties in museums such as Cox's or Lever's; and any number of public lectures or readings. When all of these venues were open to the public, the front pages of newspapers such as the *Public Advertiser* and the *Morning Chronicle* prioritized the Theatres Royal by placing their advertisements at the top of the first column, but the advertisements themselves, especially those for Sadler's Wells, appeared in a format similar to those used by the "major" houses, often listing titles, major performers, or both. Throughout King's tenure at the Wells, the *Morning Chronicle* also printed descriptions of new pantomimes and the lyrics of new musical entertainments, thereby providing coverage similar to that afforded a new play at Drury Lane. When those advertisements included the names of company members, potential audience members could readily follow performers from a Theatre Royal to a "minor" house. Thus, even if the major houses were privileged, the public would be able to recognize interplay between the venues. When

King assumed management of the Wells, a related assumption came into play: King's own identity as a performer at Drury Lane.

Thomas King addressed the public as the voice of management at Sadler's Wells in a statement published in the February 8, 1772, edition of the *Public Advertiser*. In that statement, King addressed what he called "several vague and contradictory reports" related to changes in the upcoming season. In discussing these rumors, King told the public, "that the General Entertainment will, in its Kind, vary little from that heretofore exhibited."[2] At nearly the same time, the *General Evening Post* printed the following item: "Some of the newspapers have published letters to Mr. King, the celebrated comedian, desiring the exhibition of plays at Sadler's Wells, without considering that such performances are expressly prohibited by act of Parliament."[3] These items allowed audiences to expect a renegotiated identity for Sadler's Wells, one enabled by King's assumption of management and proprietorship: the promise of no change in the "General Entertainment" both quells any anxieties related to that change and plants the notion for the possibility of change. The direct mention of a request for "the exhibition of plays" at a place where such entertainments were "expressly prohibited by act of Parliament" provides a similar affirming denial. Already a producer of pantomimes, a theatrical form also produced at Drury Lane and Covent Garden, and with the new figure of its management, "the celebrated comedian" Thomas King of Drury Lane, Sadler's Wells could then adopt the image or posture of the "major" houses without actually changing the repertory. In a similar sense, King's constant presence as the visible and active manager of Sadler's Wells also invoked the Garrick blend.

The reputation of Sadler's Wells rose quickly, and newspapers attributed that change directly to King. In particular, the *Morning Chronicle* linked an increased quality of entertainment to King. Under the prior management of Thomas Rosoman, pantomimes had been "rough and unpolished," a place where "the fathers of children came with their families, to laugh and wonder under a rough covering, at the marvelous exploits of the famous Turk, and other actors of agile sports." However, under King's leadership, the Wells had taken on a new character:

> The original view of pleasing children is still pursued; but although the feast of the eye is amply gratified, parents who, in true sincerity of heart, are lovers of the entertainment at Sadler's Wells, are no longer necessitated to excuse their being seen there, by awkwardly saying, "They came to please their children." There is now a mixture of the rational with the pleasing. Music and words, which would grace a theatre of the highest style, are nightly to be heard at the Wells; and the improved idea, the alteration in the

> species of exhibition at this place of amusement, as begot in the minds of the public, is visible from the amazing overflow of box company on Thursday evening; upwards of fifty carriages being, as we are credibly informed, obliged to return back with their contents for want of room.[4]

Thomas King had improved the quality of the allowed entertainment, possibly even breaking his promise not to change "the General Entertainment." Additionally, his presence as a visible manager provided the *Morning Chronicle* the basis for a direct comparison with the Theatres Royal, a comparison that placed Sadler's Wells on an equal footing with theatres "of the highest style." While the claim to have turned away fifty carriages might reasonably be considered puffery, this newspaper item extends into 1773 what had already been less directly created in 1772: the association of Sadler's Wells with legally recognized theatres, an association enabled by Thomas King's presence as manager.

A similar set of assumptions emerged when Sheridan gave King managerial duties at Drury Lane in 1782. In late July, both the *Morning Chronicle* and the *Morning Herald* announced that management at Drury Lane for the coming season "is left entirely in the hands of Mr. King; who, it is said, has either purchased a share in the patent, or has in his agreement with them a power so to do at a state price, whenever it shall be found agreeable or convenient to himself."[5] Although the level of King's financial involvement remained uncertain in the press, these items identified him clearly as a manager with a Garrick-like authority. This linkage of management and proprietorship is notable, particularly since King's status as proprietor had yet to solidify. The newspapers published a number of preseason items, each of which either advised King as to how Drury Lane should be run or chided him for losing performers to Covent Garden. Similar tempests of speculation preceded other seasons, but the narrative that emerged in the closing months of the 1782 summer season described a tendency to delay finalizing contracts, to allow opportunities to pass, and, in short, to fail. King's abilities—which had so elevated the status of Sadler's Wells—were not in evidence as he attempted to do the same for Drury Lane. King offered no public explanation in the press, but the additional step of obtaining approval from the proprietors, Sheridan in particular, probably caused the delays that led to that failure. However, King's actions as manager—in particular his silence regarding his actual authority—allowed the public to find the Garrick blend where it did not in fact exist.

With the apparent aim of clarifying his role in Drury Lane management, King wrote and performed a "dramatic Oglio" during the first five nights of the season. Although no newspaper printed this monologue, several described the nature of the piece. The *Morning Chronicle* provided the following interpretation: "It consisted of a whimsical medley of altered quotation from Shakespeare, and irregular comic poetry, obviously prepared for the purpose of telling the Town, by the mouth of Tom King himself, that he had ventured to undertake the management of the Old Playhouse; that, though different descriptions of persons might entertain various doubts of his ability, there should exist no ground for imputing any remissness of intention to him; and that his chief wish was to treat the Performers with all the friendship of fraternal feeling, and the Publick with all the respect arising from the deepest sense of duty and obligation."[6] While both the *Morning Chronicle* and the *Morning Herald* found the Oglio praiseworthy and recorded enthusiastic applause from Drury Lane audiences, not every newspaper reported with the same tone. The *Gazetteer and New Daily Advertiser* attributed a different intention for performing the piece. Although acknowledging that the Oglio "represent[ed] opinions and suppositions concerning the new Manager," the writer for the *Gazetteer* stated that "the town [had] not been at the trouble of forming" such thoughts. Instead, this author claimed that, the prior decade at Sadler's Wells notwithstanding, King had yet to prove whether he was "capable of animating dramatic talents, and substituting manly and elegant compositions for futile pantomimes, which have infested the Theatres under the denominations of Comedies and Tragedies." The *Gazetteer*'s commentary on King concluded by acknowledging, "On the whole, with regard to the new Manager, we have our hopes and wishes, but not unmingled with apprehensions."[7]

This short statement expresses the assumption of negative influence, or, at best, an expectation of continued mediocrity. While the equation of the character of ideal comedies and tragedies as "manly and elegant compositions" might provide the basis for viewing the legal status of the patent houses as distinct institutions in the public mindset, the depiction of the offerings at Drury Lane and Covent Garden as "futile pantomimes" also associates the "major" houses with Sadler's Wells to some extent, thus acknowledging the interplay between the major and minor houses. King's reputation as an effective producer of pantomime at the Wells both qualified him as a manager and raised apprehensions related to the status of Drury Lane's quality. Instead of the presumed stability of the Garrick blend, King's years in Drury Lane management were marked from the start as unstable and open to unwelcome change.

Over the course of four seasons, this very instability faded and reemerged within the press. More than once, writers questioned the extent of King's authority: one item identified King as "a" manager, not "the" manager.[8] At the beginning of the 1788–1789 season, King left both Drury Lane and London without advance notice in the press. Some weeks later, an "Address to the Public" written by King appeared in the *Morning Chronicle*, the *Morning Post*, and the *Public Advertiser*. Within that letter, King attempted to describe the nature of his managerial assignment, noting the lack of clearly defined authority: "[T]here has been, for some few years past, something undefined, if not undefinable, in my situation; the consequences of which have been, that I have sustained many inconveniences, and have been liable to very disagreeable attacks."[9] He noted that authors had complained to him regarding plays that had been promised production (although not by him), that performers had objected to being rejected by him even when he had no authority to employ them, and that audiences had lamented the low number of plays in the current repertory. King did not deny that these were managerial tasks; in asserting that these duties were beyond his authority, King denied the title to which these tasks were attached: "I was not Manager; for I had not the power by my agreement, nor indeed had I the wish, to approve or reject any dramatick work, the liberty of engaging, encouraging, or discharging any one performer, not sufficient authority to command the cleaning of a coat, or adding, by way of decoration, a yard of copper lace: both which, it must be allowed, were often much wanted."[10]

Having repeated the duties that were beyond his authority, King refused to proceed further into specific cases. His objective in writing the address, he continued, was not to blame others but to justify his own actions. With that stated, King then defined his duties as he understood them:

> I was to bring before the publick eye, in the best manner I could, under certain limitations, such pieces and performers as should be approved by the said proprietors: I was to negociate between party and party in forming engagements: to be generally ready to answer the publick on any complaint, disturbance &c during the time of performance: to make (subject to the controul of the patentees,) the best arrangements I could as to the order of presenting the plays in use, and to instruct such young or other performers as might be likely to derive advantage from a knowledge, which partiality was pleased to allow I had acquired, by many years observation and considerable practice.[11]

King was particularly careful to indicate the lack of authority he had possessed over the past four seasons. Had King's position been understood by the general public, such an explanation or definition would not have been necessary. He could certainly have offered such an explanation sooner. The majority of theatrical reporting would have been beyond King's control, particularly when negative items found their way into print. However, when criticisms of his policies at Sadler's Wells had arisen, King had responded by sending a letter to one or more of the newspapers. While at Drury Lane, he responded to no direct challenge regarding his management of the patent house, nor did he attempt to define his authority through a published letter prior to his resignation.

Histories that include King's address to the public tend to use it as evidence of Sheridan's aloof proprietorship, particularly after his election to Parliament,[12] but this letter provides some insight into audience reception of management. As this brief foray into the newspaper record has shown, audience perception of a restored Garrick blend at Drury Lane was accompanied by an acknowledgment of the interplay between the patent houses and the larger entertainment industry. Audiences could ignore the implications of changing managers by perceiving no change in the managerial function, or they could assume a dynamic change if the managerial function was redefined for them. Given silence, audiences found the Garrick blend.

Notes

1. Dougald MacMillan, "David Garrick, Manager: Notes on the Theatre as a Cultural Institution in England in the Eighteenth Century," *Studies in Philology* 45 (1948): 630–46. A similar assumption informs *David Garrick: Director* by Kalman A. Burnim (Pittsburgh: University of Pittsburgh Press, 1961).

2. *Public Advertiser,* February 8, 1772, 1.

3. *General Evening Post (London),* February 6–8, 1772, 4.

4. *Morning Chronicle,* May 27, 1773, 3.

5. *Morning Chronicle,* July 19, 1782, 2; *Morning Herald,* July 20, 1782, 3.

6. *Morning Chronicle,* September 18, 1782, 3.

7. *Gazetteer and New Daily Advertiser,* September 20, 1782, 3.

8. *Morning Post,* October 4, 1784, 2. The author of this item noted that the entire company seemed to be managing Drury Lane, perhaps due to King's character as an appeaser.

9. All quotations from King's letter will be from the following sources: *Morning Chronicle,* October 8, 1788, 3; *Morning Post,* October 8, 1788, 2; *Public Advertiser,* October 9, 1788, 3–4.

10. Ibid.

11. Ibid.

12. Philip H. Highfill Jr., Kalman A. Burnim, and Edward A. Langhans, *A Biographical Dictionary of Actors, Actresses, Musicians, Dancers, Managers and Other Stage Personnel in London, 1660–1800,* vol. 9 (Carbondale: Southern Illinois University Press, 1983), 31.

Image-Makers and Their Discontents

Lady Gregory and the Abbey Theatre Audience

Michael Jaros

In Ireland we are not a statue-building people. Few of our immortals live either in stone or bronze.
—*The Nation*, 1888

TEN YEARS after *The Nation* made this declaration,[1] a wave of statue madness indeed spread across Ireland in anticipation of the centenary celebrations of the 1798 Rising against the British. As statues to the "immortals" of 1798 went up across the country, the huge, public events that often developed around the dedication of these bronze and stone images began to compete with the rich tradition of the Irish oral ballad and the political speech for cultural currency. More than a general passion for civic memorial was at work here: various nationalist groups were competing for the potential energy this revered, yet failed, rising might have for their present political interests. History and its representation became very palpable things in a high-stakes game over the ownership of Ireland's cultural memory. As poet W. B. Yeats wrote at the time of the 1798 commemorations, "Ireland was appealing to the past to escape from the confusion of the present."[2] Indeed, a "confusion" of nationalist-leaning groups with different agendas and ideas vied to determine just what the Irish "nation" might become. Appeals to the past would take varied forms—from memorial parades, to ballads, to dramas—but what I would like to focus upon here is the tension between forms of performance associated with the past and the image-makers of those forms.

In 1909, Lady Augusta Gregory wrote *The Image,* a play now omitted from most theatre histories of the period.[3] My contention is that this often-neglected play, which centers on a failed attempt to create a memorial, offers a unique opportunity to study the effects various audiences had on Gregory's dramaturgy. Through my investigation of several of her works, culminating with *The Image,* I hope to highlight an anxiety made manifest during the wave of nationalist sentiment that swept turn-of-the-century Ireland, specifically the tension between more "open" forms of performance that allowed more liberty with regard to audience behavior (such as memorial procession and melodrama) and the literary modernism of the Abbey and Lady Gregory. As Susan Bennett has aptly noted, audiences themselves "read according to the scope and means of culturally and aesthetically constituted interpretive processes,"[4] and turn-of-the-century Ireland offered a variety of modes of performance participation apart from the "proper" practices traditionally associated with literary modernism.

Gregory, one of the more famous figures of the Irish Literary Revival, was mindful of the cultural import of the centenary: she had written extensively about the rich, nationalist tradition of folk ballads. She did not, however, spend 1898 processing with the crowds through Dublin, or commissioning statues, but helped instead to found the Irish Literary Theatre (in 1899), which would go on to become the Abbey and later the "National" Theatre of Ireland. She was, however—along with the directorate of Edward Martyn, William Butler Yeats, and George Moore—quite interested in becoming an "image-maker," as she put it, but in a field more closely linked to the rich tradition of oral performance in Ireland than was cold, chiseled marble or (perhaps even more alarmingly) the immense, sometimes unruly crowds that gathered around the laying of foundation stones for these monuments. The oft-quoted founding charter of the Irish Literary Theatre laid out its perceived role as a sort of educational memory machine for Dublin audiences:

> We hope to see certain plays performed in Dublin . . . which whatever their degree of excellence will be written with a high ambition, and so to build up a Celtic and Irish school of dramatic literature. We hope to find in Ireland an uncorrupted and imaginative audience trained to listen by its passion for oratory, and believe that our desire to bring upon the stage the deeper thoughts and emotions of Ireland will ensure for us a tolerant welcome. . . . [W]e will show that Ireland is not the home of buffoonery and of easy sentiment, as it has been represented, but the home of an ancient idealism. We are confident of the support of all Irish people, who are weary of misrepresentation, in carrying out a work that is outside all the political questions that divide us.[5]

Enclosed in this document are a number of assumptions about popular forms of performance, and a not-so-suppressed desire to "educate" Irish audiences on how to receive and consume their theatre. In opposition to the stereotypical Stage Irishman—drunk, blustering, buffoonish, a "scarecrow of the mind," as Gregory had called him[6]—the Irish

Literary Theatre would stage an ancient, ideal Ireland that would, it was assumed, be supported by the good will and patient, quiet appreciation of all the Irish people.

Such sentiments in fact indicated a dismissal—even a willful ignorance—of the various, and at times confrontational, forms of popular performance at work in the Irish capital and elsewhere: collective events where image-makers were not always the ones calling the tune for the crowds, despite their efforts. The push-pull of these theatrical events was a vital part of premodernist forms of audience behavior, which were very much the norm up until the very end of the nineteenth century, as the work of Neil Blackadder has aptly demonstrated.[7] This less-than-silent or -orderly behavior also included various street processions (such as the Wolfe Tone memorial parade through Dublin in 1898 [discussed below] and the "funeral" for the British Empire organized by nationalist icon Maud Gonne as a counter-performance to Queen Victoria's Diamond Jubilee in 1897), as well as the Queens and Gaiety Theatres, the largest houses in Dublin for music hall and melodrama ("buffoonery and easy sentiment"), respectively. Melodrama, the province of so many Stage Irishmen of yesteryear, was the most popular theatrical fare in Dublin at the time of the 1898 centenary and continued to be so well into the tenure of the Abbey itself. Performances became collective events where (as Mary Trotter notes), audiences regularly "hissed the villain, cheered the hero, yelled advice to the characters and sang patriotic songs."[8]

The "passion for oratory" that theatre directors hoped to harness in reality seemed fed by such theatrical events and the "melodramatic tactics," as Elaine Hadley has dubbed them, that they both lent to and shared with the orators of those various, nationally minded political discourses.[9] The main event of the centenary itself (1898) would be a gigantic funeral procession for the slain leader of the 1798 Rising, Wolfe Tone (one hundred years too late), featuring the foundation stone for a statue as a surrogate for his absent body, driven with appropriate pomp and circumstance through the streets of Dublin to St. Stephen's Green. The Yeatsian "confusion of the present" reared its ugly head, as various national image-makers fought both for position on the platform and the right to call the tune as to what Tone "meant" to the fractious groups that collectively represented Irish nationalism in 1898. Despite Gonne making a trip to America to drum up support, funds never materialized for the statue, so it was never built. The crowds dissipated and the monument was forgotten. It became more poignant in its absence, a sort of cautionary monument to a failed consensus—a lesson learned, perhaps, about how such mass, populist celebrations were not top-down, easily guidable affairs, and never could be.

Whereas Joyce comically immortalized this absence in the "Wandering Rocks" chapter of *Ulysses* (set six years after the parade), where he has Miss Dunne listlessly gaze across the vista of St. Stephen's Green, her eyes resting briefly upon the "place where Wolfe Tone's statue was not,"[10] Gregory's own writings of the time betray a deep ambivalence on her part about all this fractious popular commemoration, this talk of marching and monuments. She wrote to Yeats that if the 1798 rebellion had "worked as intended, we should now be celebrating it,"[11] and that people a century after the rising should just "plant a tree and get on with their lives"[12] versus indulging in such massive street demonstrations—the largest in Dublin since the dedication of the O'Connell monument fifteen years before—all in the name of Tone's still unfinished revolution.

This ambivalence is partially explained by her tenuous position as an Ascendancy landlord: patron of the arts and folk history she may have been, but she was (in the eyes of many) a part of the Protestant Garrison in Ireland, the class that had ruled the land for the British since Elizabeth I and the plantations. Despite her Ascendancy roots, she had that same year (1898) written an obviously nationalist piece that concerned itself with folk memory and the long history of Irish nationalist resistance reaching back to 1798. "The Felons of Our Land," published in the *Cornhill Magazine*, got her into hot water with many of her Ascendancy friends, and may have led her to declare only a little later that she would "keep out of politics and work only for literature," and not become an Irish version of Marianne at the barricades (as Gregory saw Maud Gonne). "Private beliefs," she maintained, must be kept separate from "public pronouncements."[13]

"Felons" provides vital insight into not just what Gregory thought about the "meaning" of 1798, but more importantly into her attitude toward populist forms of performance, an attitude that carried over into the founding documents of the Irish Literary Theatre only months later. "Felons" examines the Irish ballad tradition, specifically how these songs, passed down orally, enshrine memory outside of (or without) actual monuments. Initially, her praise of the tradition is effusive, remarking upon the ballads' vast potential energy. Irish history had resorted to performance as a counternarrative to official British history: "forbidden in the national schools, it has lifted up its voice in the streets, and has sung the memory of each new movement."[14] It is certainly not far from there to the language of the theatre charter about the passion and ancient idealism that might be harnessed from Irish popular performance traditions. Seventeen ninety-eight, especially the cult of Wolfe Tone himself, holds no small place in this configuration. Gregory remarks upon the fact that no tomb had in fact been built at Bodenstown (Tone's burial site), as his is a memory more aptly carried on in processions and ballads. Chief among these is the work of Thomas Davis, whom she quotes at length:

> In Bodenstown churchyard there is a green grave
> And freely around it let winter winds rave
> Far better they suit him—the ruin and the gloom
> Till Ireland, a nation, can build him a tomb.[15]

Gregory dwells upon the messianic future tense of this ballad. However, she goes on to voice her skepticism about the *low* nature of these performances, privileging first and foremost those that arrive in print form, such as songbooks for distribution: the fact that they are written down delivers them from doggerel. Examining a certain street ballad that links together all the hero-martyrs ("the immortals") of 1798, she qualifies her admiration, noting that it was "composed by a Dublin street singer, and, in spite of the stilted sounds of one who has learned a style from . . . pub oratory, there is something touching in the conscientious attention to detail where it concerns those whose names might be slipping out of memory."[16]

Gregory is anxious, here, to qualify the "low" form of performance for the high sentiments she wishes to examine: "ancient idealism" will lift these voices from the streets to the legitimate, *literary,* theatre house, or the British literary journal. "In a country that is not a reading country," Gregory remarks, "'Speeches from The Dock,' the last public words of political prisoners, is in its 48th edition."[17] It is the *written* archive of this rebel genealogy of performance that gives the performance, for Gregory, its legitimacy. Only a year later, as the Irish Literary Theatre was founded (1899), Yeats spoke publically about such issues, echoing Gregory that "the great mass of our people, accustomed to interminable political speeches, read little." However, dramatic literature, when performed, had the potential to eclipse street speeches and oral ballads, while also absorbing their populist energy: "in the theatre," Yeats maintained, "the mob becomes the people."[18] The "mob" of Dublin theatrical audiences, Blackadder wryly notes, did Yeats and Gregory the favor of staying away in large numbers during the early years of their theatre's existence.[19]

The image-makers of print and the legitimate stage thus had an educational, even civilizing mission not only to commit oral performance to the archive but to take its potential energy and channel it into "legitimate" performance. In the public sphere filled with so many different forms of performance that was colonial Ireland at the turn of the century, image-makers at the Irish Literary Theatre could not always rely on the given "support of all Irish people" they so desired.

Only a few years later, however, Yeats and Gregory collaborated on a short piece that *did* succeed in momentarily harnessing this potential energy of 1798 to the legitimate theatre with the play *Cathleen ni Houlihan*. Here, a half-remembered piece of folk memory surrounding the rebellion is embodied in the "Shan Van Vocht," the wrinkled old woman who is made young and given the "walk of a queen" by the sacrifice of young men for the nationalist cause. The central role was played by none other than Maud Gonne in the premiere and became a source of inspiration for many later leaders of the 1916 Rising, including its slain leader, Padraic Pearse, and Constance Markiewicz, both of whom were overcome by Gonne's performance in the title role.[20]

Clearly, then, theatre had the power to momentarily summon up cultural memory into an ephemeral community. However, the position of the image-maker in this theatrical event was at best unstable, as would be seen most famously five years later (1907) when their theatre, now calling itself the "National Theatre Society," became embroiled in the most famous riots in Irish theatre history, over Synge's *The Playboy of the Western World*. As has been extensively discussed, for nights on end, counter-performances by various groups in the form of songs, stamping, and other disruptions continued throughout the theatre.[21] During the riots, which lasted the better part of a week, the theatre was largely divided by respective seating position: the Anglo-Irish (including Gregory) sat in the more expensive stalls and the primarily Catholic nationalists remained in the pit. Many of the latter saw Synge's representation of the Western Irish in the play as a slander to the nation, which the theatre itself ironically claimed to represent.[22] In protesting the play, the pit audiences had only reverted to the more boisterous forms of audience behavior associated with parades, political speeches, and the melodrama and music hall houses. The week ended with diarist Joseph Holloway going so far as to remark that the music halls had indeed "emptied themselves out into the pit" of the Abbey.[23]

Gregory and Yeats both took stock of what had occurred. In the immediate aftermath, Gregory defended the artistic mission of the theatre above all else: "it is the fiddler who chooses the tune," she maintained, and "the public are quite willing to stay away, and if they come in they must take what is provided for them."[24] Years later, however, this "public" became the rhetorical "mob" and the battle over the *Playboy* became "a fight against mob censorship."[25] Yeats was more bitter. In an open letter to Lady Gregory in 1919, he actually tied failed monument-building to the fate of the Abbey: "You and I and Synge," he proclaimed, "have had to dig a stone for our statue and I am aghast at the site of a new quarry."[26] For both founders, the Abbey had itself become a chiseled image, and Yeats did not approve of how the "mob" had in fact received that image. He declared his intentions to pursue a wholly "unpopular" theatre of Noh-inspired symbolism, which he went on to do in the latter part of his life.

Gregory's immediate reaction was not to write in such monumental language as Yeats, nor to move away from the popular theatre, but instead to write a play for that theatre about a failed monument and a half dozen failed acts of communication. Her anxiety about the mercurial nature of popular reception became her 1909 play *The Image*. The play would premiere the same year as a revival of *Playboy,* put on as a tribute to Synge, who had passed away in March of that year.

The play concerns how *another* half-forgotten piece of folk memory leads a town to build a memorial statue to a man that never even existed. The work not only highlighted her skepticism about the 1898 commemorations but also her own feelings about popular reception and cultural memory. The fictional western Irish town decides (with a sudden influx of money) to build a monument to a certain "Hugh O'Lorra," a man whose name is taken from the side of a wrecked fishing vessel and whose history is completely the invention of the townspeople: each one is more than ready to insert him into the rebel ballad tradition Gregory knew so well. Their failed efforts to build a statue to him (the money vaporizes and the townspeople take to fighting among themselves over his origins) bore striking similarities to the Tone memorial processions a decade before, with its failed attempts at populist consensus, as well as the fighting that suffused the house of the Abbey two years before over the meaning of Synge's play for Irish culture and history.

At the heart of the play, then, are these very issues of memorial, memory, and the role of the populace in generating that memory. For Gregory, the central problem in generating a work is the image-maker's loss of control as that work enters the public sphere: the images seem to catch fire in the open air, burn, and vanish.

Such anxiety was woven into how Gregory both crafted and responded to the play's reception. In the original program she had included the Latin phrase *"Secretum meum Mihi,"* "My secret to myself." No riots rocked the Abbey on the nights that the play ran, but this remark—and the overall "message" of the play itself—confused many critics. Gregory responded in the press to Gaelic Leaguer D. P. Moran's review of the work (he had himself been confounded by the strange, prefatory remark) when she wrote: "I had given a heart secret into the keeping of each of the persons in the play. . . . Thomas Coppinger dreamed of the great monument he would make to some great man, and old Peggy of one made beautiful through long memory and death; and Malachi of one who was beyond and above earthly life. And each of these images crumbled at the touch of reality, like a wick that has escaped the flame, and is touched by *common* air."[27]

Moran, Gregory remarked, had himself worked to "bring back respect for the work of Irish hands" through his own newspaper, *The Leader,* affiliated as it was with the nationalist cause. She wondered, however, if the Ireland of 1909 was "all [he] intended it to be when [he] wrote in a little book I edited ten years ago [*Ideals in Ireland*] of a 'new Ireland rising up out of the foundations of the old, with love and not hate as its inspiration?' For you also have been an Image-maker." The ideal images of 1898 and 1899, Gregory seemed to say, crumbled in the "common air" that infused the political infighting of the succeeding decade. She went on to speak of the Abbey itself and its failure to live up to the founders' intended image: the directors of the theatre were "beginning to get some applause . . . but only they know how far it still is from the idea with which they set out."[28] As one image-maker to another, Gregory asked Moran for some acknowledgment of the combustible nature of images—whether placed on foundation stones, on the stages of theatres, or in print—when touched by the flame ignited by their audiences. No theatre of consensus had arrived by 1910, just as no culture of consensus had come to colonial Ireland. For Gregory, these images (statues, plays, and written works) vaporized, desiccated, or were perverted when they entered the flame of popular reception, specifically among the fractious audiences of turn-of-the-century Ireland. Gregory's own experiences as an image-maker seemed to have led her to a conclusion that was the inverse of Yeats's original idea for the Abbey: in that theatre and its history of crafting images, the people, in fact, became the mob.

Notes

1. Quoted in Luke Gibbons, "Where Wolfe Tone's Statue Was Not: Joyce, Monuments and Memory," in *History and Memory in Modern Ireland,* ed. Ian McBride (Cambridge: Cambridge University Press, 2001), 154.

2. Quoted in Gary Owens, "Nationalist Monuments in Ireland, c 1870–1914: Symbolism and Ritual," in *Ireland: Art into History,* ed. Raymond Gillespie and Brian P. Kennedy (Dublin: Town House, 1994), 106.

3. Christopher Morash mentions the play in a sentence, *A History of Irish Theatre: 1601–2000* (Cambridge: Cambridge University Press, 2002), 162; Lionel Pilkington does not mention it at all, nor does Robert Welch, in an actual history of the Abbey itself, *The Abbey Theatre 1899–1999: Form and Pressure* (Oxford: Oxford University Press, 1999); Christopher Murray, however, gives the play an

entire paragraph, claiming it was a "personal favorite" of Gregory's and that within it the "Irish fidelity to the dream image is both celebrated and mocked," *Twentieth-Century Irish Drama: Mirror up to Nation* (Syracuse, NY: Syracuse University Press, 1997), 51–52.

4. Susan Bennett, *Theatre Audiences: A Theory of Production and Reception*, 2nd ed. (London: Routledge, 1997), 92.

5. Lady Augusta Gregory, *Our Irish Theatre* (London: G. P. Putnam's Sons, 1913), 8–9.

6. Ibid., 115.

7. Neil Blackadder, *Performing Opposition: Modern Theatre and the Scandalized Audience* (London: Praeger, 2003), 2.

8. Mary Trotter, *Ireland's National Theatres: Political Performance and the Origins of the Irish Dramatic Movement* (Syracuse, NY: Syracuse University Press, 2001), 123.

9. Elaine Hadley, *Melodramatic Tactics: Theatricalized Dissent in the English Marketplace* (Stanford, CA: Stanford University Press, 1995), 3. Most famous in the Irish political context would be the long tradition of the speech from the courtroom dock, which was made by successive generations of nationalists, and was often framed in melodramatic rhetoric. See especially *The Field Day Anthology of Irish Writing*, ed. Seamus Deane (Derry, Northern Ireland: Field Day Pub., 1991), vol. 1, 933–39; vol. 2, 209–302.

10. James Joyce, *Ulysses: Annotated Student Edition*, ed. Declan Kiberd (London: Penguin, 1992), 294.

11. Quoted in R. F. Foster, *W. B. Yeats, A Life. Vol. 1: The Apprentice Mage* (Oxford: Oxford University Press, 1997), 193.

12. Quoted in R. F. Foster, "Remembering 1798," in *History and Memory in Modern Ireland*, 80.

13. Judith Hill, *Lady Gregory: An Irish Life* (Phoenix Mill, UK: Sutton, 2005), 146.

14. Lady Augusta Gregory, "The Felons of Our Land," *Cornhill Magazine*, May 1900, 624.

15. Ibid.

16. Ibid., 625.

17. Ibid., 623.

18. Quoted in P. J. Matthews, *Revival: The Abbey Theatre, Sinn Fein, the Gaelic League and the Co-Operative Movement* (Notre Dame: University of Notre Dame Press, 2003), 18.

19. Blackadder, *Performing Opposition*, 72.

20. Lionel Pilkington, *Theatre and the State in Twentieth-Century Ireland: Cultivating the People* (London: Routledge, 2001), 32.

21. See especially Blackadder, *Performing Opposition*, which contains a chapter on Synge and the riots, 69–108.

22. Blackadder, *Performing Opposition*, 75.

23. Quoted in Blackadder, *Performing Opposition*, 87.

24. Quoted in Trotter, *Ireland's National Theatres*, 125.

25. Gregory, *Our Irish Theatre*, 115.

26. W. B. Yeats, *The Collected Works of W. B. Yeats: Vol. 8: The Irish Dramatic Movement,* ed. Mary Fitzgerald and Edward J. Finneran (New York: Scribner, 2003), 131.

27. Gregory, "Notes Written for First Edition, 1910," in *The Image and Other Plays* (New York: Knickerbocker, 1922), 98. My emphasis.

28. Ibid., 98–99.

Anxious Audiences and the Early Modern English Transvestite Theatre

Robert I. Lublin

INTERSECTING the interests of theatre historians, New Historicists, and feminist scholars, the early modern English convention of having boys play the women's roles has proven a compelling subject of analysis, drawing considerable attention over the last thirty years. Despite the broad range of methodologies employed to address the issue, one aspect of cross-gender casting has not been fully considered: the importance of audiences. This is significant because our understanding of the convention during the early modern period is tightly connected to the practice of spectatorship. To begin with, extant historical responses by those who attended the theatre inform our notion of how cross-gender casting was understood at the time. Additionally, along more theoretical lines, audiences, in the act of engaging the convention, helped to construct its meaning. Within theatre studies, we needn't invoke Barthes's notion of the "death of the author" to acknowledge the importance of audiences to the making of meaning in a performance.[1] I plan briefly to survey the responses to cross-gender casting that came out of the period. Then, I wish to reflect upon the nature of the available evidence to consider the range of arguments it supports. Finally, I hope to consider how audience responses shaped the experience of cross-gender casting when it was employed in performances of early modern English drama.

Despite the extraordinary amount of recent scholarship devoted to the topic, the practice of having boys play the women's roles actually elicited very little commentary at the time. In his book *Playgoing in Shakespeare's London,* Andrew Gurr attempts to record all of the significant comments on the theatre that survive from the period. Among the wide variety of references to playgoing Gurr has unearthed, discussion (or even mention) of the ubiquitous practice of having boys play the women's parts is almost conspicuously absent.[2] That stated, the convention did elicit responses, rather strong ones, from a particular demographic: individuals who found the practice opprobrious. Antitheatrical writers published a number of tracts during the early modern period that attacked the institution of theatre, and some of them specifically mention the iniquity of transvestite drama in the theatrical enterprise. The primary members of this group are Stephen Gosson, John Rainoldes, and William Prynne.[3]

The commentaries these writers offer on the theatrical practice of cross-gender casting are not identical, but share the general opinion that the convention breaks with religious orthodoxy and inappropriately inspires lust in the observer. Gosson, for instance, in *Plays Confuted in Five Actions* (1582), first invokes the argument from Deuteronomy (22:5), which states that men who put on the apparel of women are an abomination to the Lord. He takes this further by arguing that, if merely wearing a woman's apparel is damnable, how much worse is the actor who puts on "not the apparrell onely, but the gate, the gestures, the voyce, the passions of a woman?"[4] In *Th' Overthrow of Stage-Playes* (1599), Dr. John Rainoldes, a leading Oxford divine, argues that having boys play the part of women inspires sexual desire in the audience. "The appareil of wemen is a great provocation of men to lust and leacherie . . . A womans garment beeing put on a man doeth vehemently touch and moue him with the rememberance and imagination of a woman; and the imagination of a thing desirable doth stirr up the desire."[5] Dressed as a woman, a male actor stirs up lust by provoking the audience's imagination and memory of a woman. Rainoldes further asserts that the spectator experiences homoerotic lust for the boy beneath the apparel: "an effeminate stage-player, while he faineth love, imprinteth wounds of love."[6] William Prynne, in *Histriomastix* (1633), expands upon the fear that cross-dressed boys would elicit homoerotic desire: "players and play-haunters in their secret conclaves play the sodomites; together with some modern examples of such, who have been desperately enamored with players' boys thus clad in woman's apparel, so far as to solicit them by words, by letters, even actually to abuse them."[7] Taken together, Gosson, Rainoldes, and Prynne argue that theatre is erotic and inspires uncontrollable sexual desire either for women who are invoked by the actor's apparel or for the boys who wear it.[8] It follows that those audience members who shared these antitheatrical views of a transvestite stage found sexual excitement, particularly homoerotic excitement, to be the cornerstone of the theatrical experience. But how widely held were the opinions voiced by these writers?

Surveying the field of antitheatrical writers, Lisa Jardine has stated that "amongst those who opposed [the theatres], transvestism on stage was a main plank in the anti-stage polemic."[9] If this were true, we could investigate the popularity of antitheatrical tracts to determine the pervasiveness of their arguments in English society.[10] However, quite the opposite appears to be the case. Only four antitheatrical tracts explicitly mention cross-gender casting on the stage at all (I have not listed one early, anonymous tract that reiterates the prohibition made in Deuteronomy). Most antitheatrical tracts, including those written by John Northbrook, Phillip Stubbes, Anthony Munday, and others, attack the theatre but make no mention of the practice of having boys play the female roles. Standard tropes of antitheatrical polemic were that it teaches immorality, allures the senses rather than improving the mind, encourages flouting of the sumptuary laws, and serves as a meeting place for whores and their customers.[11] The tracts quoted here by Gosson, Rainoldes, and Prynne devote literally hundreds of pages to attacking the theatre but vastly fewer to the practice of cross-gender casting. Far more pernicious and more frequently attacked is the practice of cross-dressing in society. For instance, the often-mentioned tracts *Haec Vir* and *Hic Mulier,* which directly attack men who dress in women's fashions and women who wear the apparel of men, never once mention cross-dressing for the theatre. On numerous occasions, scholars have mentioned these works when addressing drama, but such conflations must be undertaken with care. After all, the liminal nature of the theatre allows it to engage in actions that are not typically permitted in normative society.

Additionally, the attack on masculine women and effeminate men in the antitheatrical tracts actually finds echoes in the plays of the time. In Ben Jonson's *Epicoene,* for instance, a group of women called "the collegiates" are made the butt of humor for their decision to dress and act in a decidedly masculine manner. Accordingly, the cross-dressing that occurs metatheatrically (boys playing the women's roles) is permitted, while the cross-dressing that occurs within the context of the play's narrative is comically ridiculed.

Early modern English antitheatrical attacks on transvestite theatre were, therefore, shockingly rare when we consider how much attention they have received from scholars. We cannot assume that their argument regarding the sexual and homoerotic nature of theatre was widely held by audiences at the time. However, it must be noted that this position is corroborated by some evidence from plays of the time. In Jonson's *Poetaster* (1601), a father worries that his son's decision to write for the theatre will lead to sex with men: "What shall I have my sonne a stager now? an enghle [favorite] for players?"[12] Middleton similarly suggests the sexual desirability and availability of boy players in *Father Hubburd's Tales* (1604), in which a young gentleman is encouraged "to call in at the Blackfriars where he should see a nest of boys able to ravish a man."[13] Coming from individuals who worked within the theatrical enterprise, Jonson's and Middleton's statements lend credibility to Rainoldes's and Prynne's conclusion that using cross-dressed boys to play the part of women incited homoerotic desire in their audiences.

Complicating the situation, evidence supporting the opposite conclusion also exists. In Lady Mary Wroth's prose romance *The Countess of Montgomery's Urania* (1621), the experience of watching a boy play a woman's part is presented merely as one of appreciating dramatic action. In this configuration, the practice of cross-gender casting is divorced entirely from sexual desire: "there hee [her first lover] saw her with all passionate ardency, seeke, and sue for the strangers love; yet he [the stranger] unmoveable, was no further wrought, then if he had seene a delicate playboy acte a loving womans part, and knowing him a boy, lik'd onely his action."[14]

As it is figured here, the boy playing a woman's role is protected from inciting lust precisely by the convention of cross-gender casting. Precluding women from performance serves, therefore, to safeguard the stage from sexual desire. Thomas Nashe supports this notion of cross-gender casting and the morality of the English stage in *Pierce Penilesse his Supplication of the Divell* (1592): "Our Players are not as the players beyond Sea, a sort of squirting baudie Comedians, that haue whores and common Curtizens to playe womens partes, and forbeare no immodest speech, or vnchast action that may procure laughter" (Chambers 1923, 4.239).[15] Nashe suggests that the threat of sexualizing the English stage is quelled by restricting women from performance. Not only homoerotic lust, but heterosexual desire as well is contained by having the women's parts played by boys.

Thomas Heywood specifically targets and counters the arguments of antitheatrical writers when he states that the custom of cross-gender casting was a moral one with a respectable tradition in his *An Apology for Actors* (1612): "To see our youth attired in the habit of women. [W]ho knows not what their intents be? Who cannot distinguish them by their names, assuredly knowing that they are but to represent such a lady, at such a tyme appointed? Do not the universities, the fountains, and well springs of all good arts, learning and documents, admit the like in their colleges? [A]nd they (I assure myself) are not ignorant of their use. In the time of my residence at Cambridge, I have seen tragedyes, comedyes, historyes pastorals and shows publickly acted, in which the graduates of good place and reptutation have bene specially parted."[16] The dressing of boys in women's clothing, Heywood argues, serves only to represent women. Far from inspiring inappropriate desire, the practice of cross-gender casting is an ethical exercise that derives from the venerable practices of the universities.

How, then, are we to evaluate audience responses to the early modern English transvestite stage? For some, cross-dressing by male actors was a scandalous source of homoerotic attraction. For others, it was the logical, moral alternative to the practice of having women perform on stage. While there is no such thing as a unified audience response, can we go further than to note simply one extreme and its opposite?

One aspect of the available data that deserves greater consideration and offers insight into the issue is the extraordinary dearth of it. Considering the seventy-five years that separate 1567, when the first professional playhouse was built in England, and 1642, when the professional playhouses were closed by an act of Parliament, the amount of evidence touching on cross-gender casting is positively diminutive. Four antitheatrical tracts touch on the subject, with decades separating some of their publication dates. Additionally, only two plays support similar positions. And three additional sources touch on the issue but offer opposing views. Taken together, this evidence presents a very mixed message regarding audience responses to cross-gender casting. However, considering just how infrequently the issue was addressed in any form, we can reasonably conclude that the practice of cross-gender casting did not inspire a great deal of anxiety in the audience members who consistently experienced it in the theatre.

Whether or not audience members found the cross-dressed boys to be a source of sexual desire, very few found them to be a source of significant concern or interest. Instead, cross-gender casting seems to have simply been accepted in England as the norm of theatrical representation.[17] Juliet Dusinberre puts the convention in perspective when she asks: "Were [women] there or not? Of course, physically they were not there. But to assert that is, in my view, to say nothing. Because none of the shadows on Shakespeare's stage are there. There are no kings, queens, murderers, monsters, fairies, politicians, wise counselors, or even fools. There are only actors. Why should it matter that they are not biologically female, any more than it should matter that they are not royal, Roman, Moors, Egyptian, or Italian?"[18]

Theatre is an art of conventions. Accordingly, Kathleen McLuskie is surely right to conclude that, on some level, boy actors playing women must have simply been accepted by the great majority of theatregoers as a convention.[19] Otherwise, audiences would have been unable to engage the dramatic narratives that are premised on heterosexual love and the differences distinguishing men from women.[20]

This does not abnegate the probability that, among the ten to twenty thousand people who attended the theatre every week in early modern England,[21] some were likely sexually drawn to the boy actors, just as some men in the audience were likely attracted to the adult male actors. Further, virtually no one has seriously considered the heterosexual desire experienced by the women who attended the theatre in significant numbers. What I wish to draw attention to is the overwhelming likelihood that the convention of cross-gender casting was not a source of profound anxiety for the early modern English society. There was no law prohibiting women from performing, and no new law was passed at the start of the Restoration to draw women to the practice of acting on stage. This apparent lack of concern regarding the convention has foiled all efforts to find a satisfying explanation for why the early modern English stage had boys play the women's parts.[22]

Consequently, it strikes me that the need to find an explanation for the convention of cross-gender casting is a decidedly late twentieth- and twenty-first-century one and did not matter significantly to the early modern English men and women who attended the theatre. Indeed, the very methodologies that have come to the fore in recent years have encouraged the issue's increased consideration. Among its various goals and methodologies, feminism seeks to interrogate the past to understand the construction of gender in history. Such a goal encourages the consideration of cross-gender casting. Similarly, New Historicism attempts to consider texts within discursive contexts. In providing discursive contexts, the antitheatrical tracts, which had a highly restricted circulation and ultimately a very limited influence upon theatre, have played a disproportionately influential role in determining our understanding of how meaning was established and received in early modern England. Thus, for both feminism and New Historicism, cross-gender casting reveals contemporary interests more than early modern ones. It follows that, even more than explicating early modern English concerns, the several dozen articles and books addressing cross-gender casting that have appeared over the last thirty years demonstrate our modern fixation on depictions of sex and gender in the theatre.

It seems reasonable to suggest that cross-gender casting is a greater source of interest and anxiety for contemporary individuals and audiences than it was in early modern England. With this in mind, it is worth considering the production of Shakespeare's *Henry V* that was used to open the new Globe in London in 1997. For this production, historically accurate costumes were constructed and dyed by hand using original materials and methods of the period. Further, all of the women's roles were played by men. The intention, director Richard Olivier explained, was to "undertake to explore certain authentic production methods or styles."[23] Performing an early modern script on a facsimile of an early modern stage using early modern apparel and engaging early modern conventions, this production of *Henry V* must have seemed as historically accurate as possible. And yet, one crucial aspect of the production was unambiguously anachronistic: the audience. Accordingly, if recent scholarship does indeed reflect heightened anxiety regarding the theatrical representation of sex and gender roles, it is likely that the late twentieth-century production of *Henry V* produced far more interest, concern, and anxiety by having boys play the women's roles than did the one staged at the original Globe in 1599.[24]

Notes

1. Roland Barthes, "The Death of the Author," in *Image/Music/Text,* trans. Stephen Heath (New York: Hill and Wang, 1977), 142–47.

2. Andrew Gurr, *Playgoing in Shakespeare's London* (New York: Cambridge University Press, 1987).

3. It has become critical commonplace to label antitheatrical writers "Puritans" since they were typically outspoken preachers, but recent commentary has shown this to be an unfair descriptor. To discuss the antitheatrical writers as a group, we do better to term them "zealots": the language they bring to bear engages morality and religion but not a specifically Puritan religiosity. Tanya Pollard, *Shakespeare's Theatre: A Sourcebook* (Malden, MA: Blackwell, 2004), 20, and Paul Whitefield White, *Theatre and Reformation: Protestantism, Patronage and Playing in Tudor England* (New York: Cambridge University Press, 1993), xiii.

4. Stephen Gosson, *Plays Confuted in Five Actions* (New York: Garland, 1972), sig. C3v.

5. John Rainoldes, *Th' Overthrow of Stage-Playes* (Middleburgh, 1599), 97.

6. Ibid., 18.

7. William Prynne, *Histriomastix* (London, 1633), 209.

8. Stephen Orgel, *Impersonations: The Performance of Gender in Shakespeare's England* (New York: Cambridge University Press, 1996), 30.

9. Lisa Jardine, "Boy Actors, Female Roles, and Elizabethan Eroticism," in *Staging the Renaissance: Reinterpretations of Elizabethan and Jacobean Drama,* ed. David Scott Kastan and Peter Stallybrass (New York: Routledge, 1991), 57.

10. Thomas Postlewait warns readers against assuming that antitheatrical tracts were widely read and accepted in early modern England: "Most pamphlets had a limited distribution, so they probably did not carry much weight with theatre audiences, many of whom were not literate." Thomas Postlewait, "Theatricality and Antitheatricality in Renaissance London," in *Theatricality,* ed. Tracy C. Davis and Thomas Postlewait (New York: Cambridge University Press, 2003), 98.

11. Jean E. Howard, *The Stage and Social Struggle in Early Modern England* (New York: Routledge, 1994), 75.

12. Ben Jonson, *The Complete Plays of Ben Jonson*, vol. 2, ed. G. A. Wilkes (Oxford: Clarendon Press, 1981), 1.2.15–16.

13. Thomas Middleton, *Father Hubburd's Tale* in *Thomas Middleton: The Collected Works*, ed. Gary Taylor and John Lavagnino (New York: Oxford University Press, 2007), ln. 559–61.

14. Lady Mary Wroth, *The Countesse of Mountgomeries Urania* (London, 1621), 60.

15. E. K. Chambers, *The Elizabethan Stage*, 4 volumes (Oxford: Clarendon Press, 1923), 4:239.

16. Ibid., 1:252.

17. Michael Shapiro, *Gender in Play on the Shakespearean Stage* (Ann Arbor: University of Michigan Press, 1994), 41.

18. Juliet Dusinberre, "Women and Boys Playing Shakespeare," in *A Feminist Companion to Shakespeare*, ed. Dympna Callaghan (Malden, MA: Blackwell, 2000), 251.

19. Kathleen McLuskie, "The Act, the Role, and the Actor: Boy Actresses on the Elizabethan Stage," *New Theatre Quarterly* 3 (1987): 121.

20. Jean Howard, "Crossdressing, the Theatre, and Gender Struggle in Early Modern England," *Shakespeare Quarterly* 39, no. 4 (1988): 435.

21. See Postlewait, "Theatricality and Antitheatricality in Renaissance London," 103.

22. Phyllis Rackin, "Shakespeare's Crossdressing Comedies," in *A Companion to Shakespeare's Works: The Comedies*, ed. Richard Dutton and Jane E. Howard (Malden, MA: Blackwell, 2003), 115.

23. Pauline Kiernan, "Findings from the Globe Opening Season: *Henry V*," *Research Bulletin* 2 (March 1998): 6.

24. I mention the 1997 production of *Henry V* here primarily to draw attention to the very different attitudes toward cross-gender casting that were maintained in early modern England. For those who wish to consider contemporary cross-gender cast performances of Shakespeare in greater depth, I recommend James C. Bulman's collection, *Shakespeare Re-Dressed: Cross Gender Casting in Contemporary Performance* (Madison, NJ: Fairleigh Dickinson University Press), 2008. The essay "Constructing Femininity in the New Globe's All-Male *Antony and Cleopatra*" by Robert Conkie directly addresses the production of *Henry V* and other cross-gender cast productions at the new Globe.

Neglected Evidence

Interpreting the Site of an Elizabethan Royal Entertainment

Paulette Marty

Scholars of Elizabethan performance have analyzed many types of evidence—from literature to visual art to archeological remains of playhouses—but have largely neglected physical evidence from extant multipurpose performance sites. Although, unlike playhouses, these extant sites are not dedicated performance spaces, examining the evidence they offer can give us important insights into the material conditions of Elizabethan performances and the perceptions of Elizabethan audiences. In this essay, I will interpret some of the physical and topographical evidence available at the site of an important Elizabethan entertainment to demonstrate how such evidence can enrich our understanding of performances in this significant period.

In July 1575, Queen Elizabeth I visited Robert Dudley, Earl of Leicester, at his castle in Kenilworth as part of her summer progress. Progresses were journeys in which the monarch and her court traveled around the kingdom, staying in towns and at the manor houses of nobles. Her hosts typically provided lodging, food, and entertainment for the court. When Elizabeth stayed at Kenilworth in 1575, Leicester spent lavishly to provide her with the most opulent, spectacular entertainment of her reign, including water pageants, mock battles, masques, and other performances. Through these spectacles, he sought to glorify and impress the Queen, but he also sought to glorify himself and impress the hundreds (perhaps thousands) of other people in attendance.

Elizabethan progress entertainments had complex audience/performer relationships. The privileged audience member was the Queen: she sat or stood at the best vantage point, the performers often addressed her directly, and most of the dialogue literally or metaphorically discussed her good qualities. But Elizabeth was a performer as well as a spectator. She performed passively by maintaining an acute awareness that the assembled crowd was watching her during the entertainments and adjusting her composure accordingly. She also performed more actively when pageants incorporated her into their fictions, either as herself or as a mythological character. Her central reason for repeatedly dragging her reluctant court out on summer progress was to engender the loyalty of her subjects by displaying herself to them in a positive light; she dutifully performed the role of majestic and benevolent monarch while the pageant players performed the roles of loyal subjects, admiring mythological figures, and wild villains smitten by the power of the Queen's majestic presence. The assembled spectators watched each of these performances and, in doing so, formed impressions of the Queen and of her hosts who sponsored the spectacles. These hosts—and the writers and performers of the entertainments—were keenly aware that their audience extended beyond the person of the Queen.

Despite this dual orientation toward both the Queen and the non-royal audience, most scholarly studies of Elizabethan royal entertainments focus on the Queen's perception and reception and neglect to examine evidence for other audience members' perceptions. This is partly because the pageant texts have a thematic preoccupation with their royal audience: when you read a dramatic text that keeps talking about and addressing the Queen, you naturally envision the Queen watching and reacting to the performance. But an overreliance on such literary evidence has led to an overemphasis on a single (admittedly important) audience member. Other types of evidence, such as records, maps, and the physical remains of the performance site, can tell us much about what the other spectators would have seen and heard and how they might have received the performances. I will illustrate how an analysis of one type of extant evidence—the physical remains of the castle and estate—can give us clues as to what the diverse audience members at Kenilworth experienced during that hot July of 1575.

The primary sources that scholars have mined most heavily for evidence of the Kenilworth entertainment are two printed texts, both published within a year after the event. *The Princely Pleasures at Kenelworth Castle* was published in 1576 and includes the texts of the pageants held during the Queen's nineteen-day stay.[1] The publication attributes authorship to George Gascoigne, but several playwrights actually contributed. *Princely Pleasures* gives the dialogue and some stage directions for the pageants, which accounted for a significant number of the total performances, but it gives no descriptions of the non-pageant performances and ceremonies. Because this text describes only the pageants, it provides the reader with a highly selective, narrow picture of the Queen's visit. The other major primary source is a letter, ostensibly written by a court official named Robert Langham.[2] Langham's *A Letter* was published in August 1575, just one month after the Kenilworth entertainment. It offers less detail on the pageants than *Princely Pleasures,* but includes descriptions of non-pageant performances, as well as ceremonies, sports, and various other happenings during Elizabeth's stay. With the wealth of rich information in these two texts, many scholars who have studied the entertainment have neglected to consult other extant, non-textual evidence.

In her study of this event, Sandra Logan critiques previous scholars for relying too heavily on literary evidence. Though she takes seriously "the 'new historicist' endeavor to recognize the entirety of material and ideological traces of the past as a field of artifacts available for interpretation in textual terms,"[3] Logan does not actually access the wide "field of artifacts available" for the Kenilworth entertainment. The "non-literary" evidence she uses is Langham's *Letter,* which she deems nonliterary because it is written in an informal prose style. While Langham's *Letter* may not fit her definition of "literature" as does Gascoigne's *Princely Pleasures,* Langham's *Letter* is a published linguistic text written by an author who was concerned with the aesthetics of his work. Logan's almost exclusive focus on these two pieces of evidence does serve her stated goal of analyzing the relationship between texts and the events they describe, but it undermines the claims she makes about the material conditions of the event, the implications of the performances, and the experiences of the audiences. She does not cite state, civic, or household records or maps in her discussion of the Kenilworth entertainment, nor does she analyze nonlinguistic artifacts, like artworks, household objects, extant buildings, or features on the Kenilworth landscape.

For one example of how our understanding of the Kenilworth entertainment can be enriched by an analysis of landscape features, I will discuss the fireworks displays that Leicester sponsored on three nights of the Queen's visit. Langham reports that these displays were lengthy—up to two hours long—and at least one was accompanied by cannon fire and could be heard and seen twenty miles away. Langham, who likely watched the fireworks from inside the castle walls, was apparently awestruck. In his description of the second display, he poetically attributes responsibility for the pyrotechnics to Jupiter and reports that the god began moderately, building in a crescendo to his full power: "with blaz of burning darts, flying too and fro, leamz of starz coruscant, streamz and hayl of fiery sparks, lyghtenings of wyldefier a water and lond, flyght and shot of thunderbollts: all with such continuauns, terrour and vehemency: that the heavins thunderd, the waters soourged, the earth shook."[4]

Langham's vivid (if somewhat fanciful) description certainly gives readers a clear and impressive image of this fireworks display. However, the image can be further enhanced when we supplement Langham's description with information about the acoustic environment of Kenilworth.

Bruce R. Smith, an Elizabethan scholar who has made extensive use of nonliterary artifacts in his work, analyzes the soundscape of Elizabethan Kenilworth in chapter 3 of *The Acoustic World of Early Modern England: Attending to the O-Factor.* Smith notes that the castle was flanked by a village, farmland, and hunting chase, so the sounds surrounding it were rural in nature: larks singing, crows cawing, farmers calling in the fields, and hunting hounds baying in the chase. In comparison to twenty-first-century Kenilworth, which features typical sounds of modern life (revving engines, amplified music, whirring hard drives), Leicester's era was very quiet. As Smith observes: "In an acoustic environment that, apart from barking dogs and the occasional gunshot, lacked any sounds above 60 decibels, all sounds would be present with an intensity quite beyond anything imaginable on the same site today."[5] Although we would have no hope of recreating that sixteenth-century soundscape in today's Kenilworth, Smith provides us with information that can help us imagine this quieter world in which the unusually loud sounds of Leicester's entertainments would have been intensely present to the assembled spectators.

In spite of the modern ambient noise on the Kenilworth estate today, one can still stand on the rise that used to be the south bank of the mere (a lake now drained), speak just above normal speaking volume, and hear a clear echo of one's voice bouncing back from the castle's edifice (see figure 1). Imagine how much louder that sound would have seemed carrying over a body of water to the sixteenth-century audience present during the Queen's visit, most of whom lived in quiet, rural environments with few large, acoustically reflective stone buildings.

Now, imagine that same audience standing in that location during one of the aforementioned fireworks displays. Fireworks and artillery fire can each make sounds over 150 decibels, so the cacophony of sound must have been overwhelming for many of the spectators, particularly when accompanied by fire brightening the night sky. The spectators on the south bank would have had an even more intense sensory experience than the Queen, who stood inside the castle, because the cannons were probably placed near them on the south bank of the mere. All the light and noise must have made for an impressive display of Leicester's power and wealth, as well as the power of his family: his brother Ambrose, earl of Warwick and the Queen's Master of the Ordnance, almost surely supplied the cannon fire.

1. View of the southern face of Kenilworth Castle from the southern bank of the former mere. Photo by author.

No matter how evocatively Langham (or any other author) describes an event like one of these fireworks displays, linguistic imagery cannot recreate a perceptual experience as rich and complex as that experienced by the spectators who actually attended the event. To discover more about the participants' perceptual experiences, we need to examine the material conditions of the performances. One of the richest sources of evidence for the material conditions of performance is the performance site itself. In cases where the site is extant, historians too often ignore the valuable evidence it offers. Theatre historians have helped shepherd and design scores of reconstructions of Elizabethan playhouses around the world in order to learn what these re-created spaces can teach us about the period. Similarly, I encourage us also to learn all we can from multipurpose Elizabethan playing spaces that still stand, such as Kenilworth Castle.

Studying the topography of a landscape like that at Kenilworth can provide us insights into how the entertainments were perceived by the spectators. For example, it is likely that Leicester, who held the important position of Master of the Horse, provided the impressive display of horsemanship included among the entertainments for the Queen's visit. Interestingly, one could read both Gascoigne and Langham's accounts and remain uncertain of the entertainment to which I refer; neither text emphasizes the equestrian skill this particular event required. The event here is the Hock Tuesday play, a traditional, civic show that had been performed by amateur and semiprofessional players in nearby Coventry since the early fifteenth century.[6] The Hock Tuesday troupe came to Kenilworth to perform their play for the Queen underneath her chamber window during the second week of her visit.

Gascoigne dismisses the Hock Tuesday play as a "countrie shewe" that was "so plaine as needeth no further explication."[7] In contrast, Langham describes the show in some detail. He relates that the play depicted a supposedly historical eleventh-century battle between local Anglo-Saxons and occupying Danes. He describes the troupe's leader, a local storyteller named Captain Cox, who probably narrated the story in between the mock battle scenes. And, most importantly for our purposes, he describes the elaborate fight choreography performed by the players. The cavalry fought first, engaging in a "hot skirmish" with spears and shields that grew into a "blazing battail" with swords, all on horseback. Langham reports that their "furious encoounterz" caused many to "tumbl too the dust, sumtime hors and man." Next came the foot soldiers, forming their ranks into precise geometric patterns as they fought. Their performance "brought all indeed into the great court" and the Queen, who saw only the tail end, was so intrigued that she ordered them to return and perform a second time, rewarding them handsomely for this second performance.

While Langham's account does paint a picture of an exciting and well-executed performance, he does not mention the element that I would argue made it especially impressive to the spectators: the location in which it was performed. Langham reports that the show took place in the castle's outer court, where the Queen could watch it from the windows of her chambers in Leicester's Building.[8] In earlier centuries, earthen fortifications, including a dry moat, had been built in this courtyard; the terrain was by then (and remains today) an undulating, uneven piece of ground (see figure 2). The Hock Tuesday players must have been highly skilled and strikingly adaptable performers to successfully transfer their play to this terrain. The horsemen's ability to safely, satisfyingly depict a mounted battle on this uneven surface next to a relatively deep dry moat testifies to their skill, as does the fact that the footmen could form identifiable geometric shapes on such irregular, unfamiliar terrain. Because Langham does not describe this topography, the only extant evidence for the contribution it may have made to the play's reception lies in the ground itself, within the walls of the castle site.

Why do some scholars fail to access this type of topographic and physical evidence for historical performances? In the cases of Sandra Logan

2. View of the outer court of Kenilworth Castle from underneath the window of the Queen's chambers. Photo by author.

and Wendy Wall, it is because their primary interests are actually Langham's and Gascoigne's texts rather than the entertainment they recount. While such study (of the relationship between a text and the event it describes) is perfectly valid, Wall becomes so invested in the impact of Gascoigne's text that she declares: "Only in the reported accounts can the full spectacular force of royal display be truly realized."[9] This assertion is text-centric almost to the point of absurdity. How can a printed text have greater "spectacular force of royal display" than a live performance in which the Queen herself, in her sumptuous clothing and jewelry, is viewed by spectators? This is akin to suggesting that reading a published transcript of Prince William and Kate Middleton's 2011 wedding in London would have been more impressive than attending the event itself. The "spectacular force" of the performances at Kenilworth (and, for that matter, at Prince William's wedding) lies not in the language spoken, nor even in the spectacle of the royals, courtiers, performers, costumes, set pieces, and props, but in the sense of occasion created by the convergence of all these elements in the presence of throngs of spectators. Repeatedly seeing Leicester, finely dressed, watching entertainments beside the Queen as he hosted her in unprecedented splendor on his estate would have affected the spectators' image of him far more than the speeches spoken by the performers.

3. Reconstruction of Kenilworth Castle as it might have appeared from the east in 1575, by Stephen Conlin. Reprinted from Richard K. Morris, *Kenilworth Castle* (London: English Heritage, 2006), 9. Used by permission of English Heritage.

One performance in which visual imagery and a sense of occasion must have affected spectators' perceptions more than spoken language was an aquatic pageant that took place the day after the Hock Tuesday play. Susan Frye has offered an oft-cited interpretation of this pageant in chapter 2 of her book, *Elizabeth I: The Competition for Representation.*[10] While Frye's interpretation is compelling, she bases it entirely upon Gascoigne's text and overlooks the extant material evidence from the castle site. By analyzing the topography and physical remains of the performance space alongside Frye's argument, we can see just how profoundly such material evidence can affect our understanding of Elizabethan audience perception and reception.

The aquatic pageant took place on July 18 on the mere, around the bridge that crossed the water to the northwest of the castle walls (see figure 3). The plot of the pageant centered on the freeing of the Lady of the Lake, who supposedly lived in the mere and had been forced to remain hidden under its waters by a besieging knight intent upon stealing her virtue. The original plan for the pageant was for Leicester to lead a small force into an elaborate mock battle with the knight. Leicester was to defeat the knight's forces and deliver the Lady of the Lake to Elizabeth, who was to watch all of this from the lakeshore. But Gascoigne tells us that the pageant was revised prior to performance. The version that was actually performed omitted the battle and recast Elizabeth as the champion responsible for defeating the besieging knight. As Elizabeth stood upon this bridge, Neptune's emissaries rode up on dolphin-shaped vessels and reported that the Queen's mighty presence had frightened away the knight. Then the Lady of the Lake herself floated up on a barge and offered thanks to Elizabeth.

Frye argues that, during the Queen's visit to Kenilworth, she was locked in competition with Leicester for control over how she was represented in his entertainments and that she used this aquatic pageant to wrest control of her representation from the earl. Frye implies that the Queen accomplished this by insisting that the pageant be changed to depict her, rather than Leicester, as a victorious champion whose virtue banished threat, while depicting Leicester merely as a powerless "observer of her power."[11] Analyzed in isolation, the pageant text supports Frye's argument; however, an additional analysis of the material conditions of the performance problematizes her conclusions.

The aquatic pageant took place at twilight as the royal party returned from hunting. The figures in the pageant floated upon the lake and approached the Queen as she crossed the wooden bridge Leicester had commissioned. This "fayr tymberd bridge" was an impressive piece of engineering and many of the assembled spectators would have been aware that it was Leicester who had sponsored its construction.[12] The spectators had a stunning view of the Queen and earl perched high upon the bridge, side-by-side on their horses. By all accounts, Leicester was an excellent horseman and cut an impressive figure when mounted. Most of the assembled spectators stood on the eastern and southern banks of the lake (see figure 4). From that perspective, the midsummer sun, setting in the northwest, would have created a burnished aura around the Queen and the earl and set the red stones of the castle—Leicester's grand seat of power—aglow. The walls of the medieval Great Hall were ornamented with radiant stained glass, illuminated by the fireplaces within. Other buildings that Leicester had built or remodeled glittered with huge sheets of clear glass, a mark of wealth and fashion in 1570s England. The performers crossed the calm water in cleverly designed boats shaped like mermaids and dolphins. The spectators (who would have included farmers, laborers, housewives, merchants, gentry, and perhaps visiting foreigners as well as court officials and courtiers) must have appreciated the beauty of this tableau, a spectacle they knew Leicester had shaped.

In contrast, not all of the spectators would have been impressed by the pageant's language, because relatively few would have been able to hear the actors' speeches. Those on the south bank of the mere were close

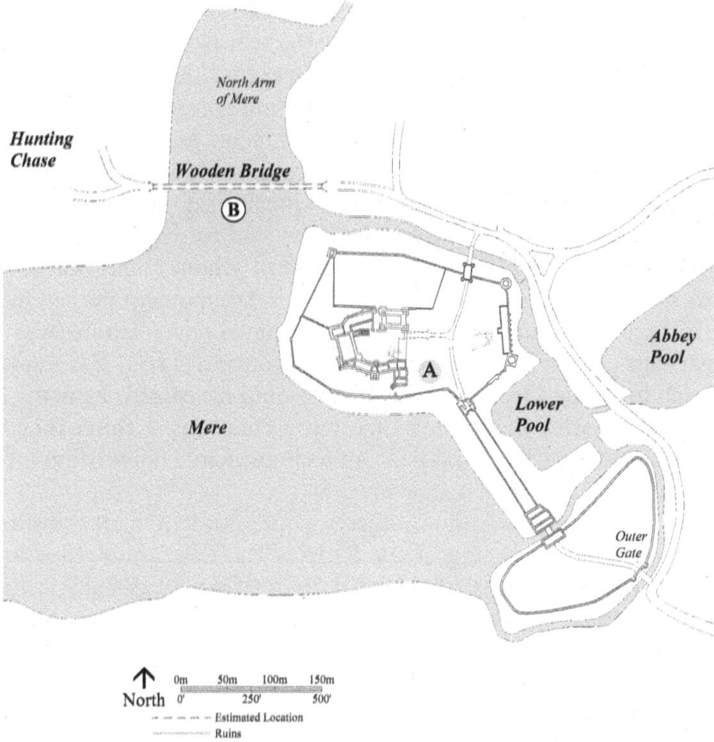

4. Map of the Kenilworth estate as it stood in 1575. Location A is the outer court where the Hock Tuesday play was performed and location B is the portion of the mere where the aquatic pageant was performed. Map by John Marty, drawing upon information from Richard K. Morris, *Kenilworth Castle* (London: English Heritage, 2006) and M. W. Thompson, *Kenilworth Castle: Warwickshire* (London: Her Majesty's Stationery Office, 1977) and "Kenilworth Castle, UK." Image. *Google Earth.* Web. July 8, 2009. Used by permission of John Marty.

enough to see the spectacle, but probably not to hear the spoken word. They were more likely to have heard the "incomparably melodioous" final song of the pageant as it resounded across the waters. According to Langham, the crowds grew silent during this last song, implying that at least some of them had been milling about and talking earlier in the pageant, which would have further prevented their fellows from hearing the speeches.[13]

In Frye's interpretation of the power differential at this moment, she takes into account only a few of the tools Leicester and Elizabeth used to shape their representations; namely, the words and blocking scripted in the pageant text. But, like all adept politicians, Leicester and Elizabeth would have used other tools as well, including constant subtle and overt adjustments to their bodies, their environment, and their spatial relationship to one another. By setting this pageant upon this bridge at this time of day and placing himself by the Queen's side, Leicester created a memorable image of himself as a glorious lord for the visual consumption of all the assembled spectators, most of whom could not hear the words spoken by the actors. Frye reads this as the moment in the Queen's visit to Kenilworth in which Leicester lost control over Elizabeth's—and by extension, his own—representation. In contrast, I read it as a moment in which both the Queen and Leicester would have used the many tools at their disposal to shape their own representations. I think they both probably rode away from this pageant feeling their "competition for representation" remained at a stalemate.

Logan asserts that common subjects would not have had access to this "little drama of the freeing of the Lady of the Lake" and refers to this and the other pageants printed in *Princely Pleasures* as "physically peripheral" because they were outside the castle walls.[14] This statement is indicative of the tendency of Elizabethan royal performance scholars to focus on the Queen's perspective to the exclusion of the perspectives of other spectators. The aquatic pageant and other performances held outside the walls may have been staged farther from the Queen's chamber than those held inside the walls, but they were visible to far more audience members; I would label them "physically accessible" rather than "physically peripheral." Those spectators on the far shore of the mere would not have been able to hear speeches or see details, but they would have been able to take in the whole visual scope of the spectacle, likely even more impressive than the individual components of the performance. And hosts like Leicester were concerned with impressing these audience members.

Although Langham and Gascoigne do not specifically describe the perspectives of the non-royal spectators, the grounds of the estate hold abundant evidence for their points of view. It is my hope that, in future studies, scholars will consider such physical evidence and thereby further enrich our understanding of the experiences of Elizabethan audiences.

Notes

1. George Gascoigne, *Complete Works,* ed. John W. Cunliffe (Cambridge: Cambridge University Press, 1910).

2. Robert Langham, *A Letter,* ed. R. J. P. Kuin (Leiden: E. J. Brill, 1983).

3. Sandra Logan, *Text/Events in Early Modern England: Poetics of History* (Aldershot: Ashgate, 2007), 6.

4. Langham, *A Letter,* 43.

5. Bruce R. Smith, *The Acoustic World of Early Modern England: Attending to the O-Factor* (Chicago: University of Chicago Press, 1999), 76.

6. Paulette Marty, "The Coventry Hock Tuesday Play: Its Origin and Relationship to Hocktide," *Medieval English Theatre* 22 (2000): 112–26.

7. Gascoigne, *Complete Works,* 106.

8. Langham, *A Letter,* 52–55.

9. Wendy Wall, *The Imprint of Gender: Authorship and Publication in the English Renaissance* (Ithaca, NY: Cornell University Press, 1993), 136–37.

10. Susan Frye, *Elizabeth I: The Competition for Representation* (Oxford: Oxford University Press, 1993).

11. Ibid., 87.

12. Langham, *A Letter,* 37.

13. Ibid., 58.

14. Logan, *Text/Events in Early Modern England,* 109, 171 n. 60.

Creating Ideal Audiences

Ludwig Tieck and German Access to Shakespeare

Natalie Tenner

Does the theatre create the audience or the audience create the theatre? Depending on the artists and on contemporary society, the power to influence the type of art created and distributed shifts between the producers and the consumers. Prior to the first unification of Germany in 1871, the early Romantic movement was in many ways focused not on actual theatregoers but on an idealized audience the artists hoped to create through their art. Particularly in the theatre, early Romantics theorized ways in which the art form could incite feelings of national unity as well as provide a moral guidepost for the audience in attendance. The potential of the theatre to mold and shape its audience was not being satisfactorily realized for many of the Romantic theorists; however, much of the contemporary German theatre was modeled after French Neoclassicism. A new form was needed that would convey the German "spirit." The Romantics turned for help to authors such as Shakespeare and Calderón; one German theatre practitioner in particular, Ludwig Tieck, went so far as to advocate Elizabethan-style performances of Shakespeare in order to create a new, "German" form of theatre. I will explore more closely the Romantics' relationship with Shakespeare, Tieck's pursuit of Elizabethan practices on the German stage, and argue that Tieck ultimately hoped, through Shakespearean performance, to create an ideal audience, unified and strengthened in its "Germanness."

Based on Tieck's own writing and on the tenets of early Romantic authors, the purpose of art (including the theatre) was not simply to entertain but also to teach. However, the ability of the artist to reach the audience went beyond a Neoclassical sense of decorum and instead aimed at the "spirit," a term that could refer to the connecting force between all humans or to the inner essence and most important aspect of a human individual. The idea of the spirit, or "character, emotion, sentiment, and soul" all referred to the "inner man," the part of the human that stands in opposition to "rational systemizing" and instead relies on nonrational processes to produce response.[1] For the early German Romantics, the effect of art on the receiving audience had two main goals: the instilling of a sense of national unity and pride and the moral improvement of the individual audience members to strengthen the whole. It did not entirely matter who the receiving audience member was when he approached a work of art—the goal was to create a "German" with a sense of national history and pride who now had the tools to make the correct decisions regarding himself and his countrymen.[2] While the undefined use of the label "German" is problematic, as is the amorphous idea "correct decisions," a closer examination of some of the ideas of the German Romantics will elucidate these goals.

The situation of the German people in the late eighteenth and early nineteenth century lent itself to debates about identity and the role of art in society. Early Romantic artists were working not as united Germans but as members of disparate German states with no common government or strong sense of cultural history. Though Tieck did not live to see Germany become a unified country in 1871, his work draws on the Romantic desire to cultivate a cultural bed from which a strong German country could grow. The desire for a unified nationality showed strongly in the artists of the Romantic movement: there was "an emphasis on 'Germanness,' a desire to uncover the cultural roots that seemed to have been overlaid by so many foreign influences."[3] For these artists, the basis of the German nation would not be military, but instead would depend on a "cultural strength": a rediscovery, or in many cases a recreation, of a German cultural history.[4] Therefore, the Germans emphasized those areas of their history that could induce pride and were recognizably "German." Much of this historical focus centered on art; the historian George Mosse suggests that German nationalism "was not concerned with boundaries or even with blueprints for a government, but with 'culture' as a whole."[5] In this period, works like Grimm's *Fairy Tales* emerged and began to take on a "national purpose."[6] Friedrich Schiller argued that if poets could join together to write about national topics, as he did in *Wilhelm Tell,* the result would be "a national stage, and we should become a nation."[7] Friedrich von Schlegel emphasized the importance of "national memories" if the German people were to unite and survive.[8]

The (re)creation of a cultural history seems to have occurred in two principal ways. The first was to look to and try to understand the people in the German states who had not been affected by the influence of other countries, particularly France. These people came to be known as the Volk, a sort of mythologized working class who revered nature and the human soul and who could trace their origins back to the Teutonic tribes that allegedly stood strong against the corruption of Ancient Rome.[9] This group embodied the ideals that existed at the very center of Romantic thought: emotion, individual freedom, the inner spirit, and nature. The emphasis shifted away from structure, hierarchy, and class; in fact, the existence of an industrial middle class raised suspicions for some nationalists.[10] The emerging construction of the Volk by artists led to a kind of folk revival that included folk songs, "folktale, saga, and myth."[11] In this crucial period of discovering and creating a cultural history, the Volk provided the links to traditional German culture, understood as access to something authentically German.

The second source of cultural inspiration came from established artists from other countries in whom the Germans saw some sort of spiritual or natural connection. In painting, the German "Nazarenes" looked to the medieval painters through Raphael; in theatre, Tieck turned to Shakespeare. The combination of a German folkloric history with appropriated artists from other countries created, for the Romantic artists, a rich cultural base that a new German nation could be proud to own and that other countries would respect.

It may seem counterintuitive for artists who were attempting to promote German national unity to model themselves after artists from other countries. In the case of Shakespeare, the explanation is precise, if not altogether comprehensible. As Tieck described it, "Shakespeare and his better contemporaries are also German."[12] Georg Gottfried Gervinius, a significant Shakespeare scholar of the early nineteenth century, claims that Shakespeare "has become a German poet almost more than our native writers."[13] This sentiment was echoed a half-century later by Gerhart Hauptmann: "There is no nation, not even the British, which is more entitled to call Shakespeare its own than Germany. Shakespeare's characters have become part of our world, his soul has become one with ours: and though he was born and buried in England it is in Germany that he is truly alive."[14] In addition, several poets in the early nineteenth century, including Tieck, paralleled Germany with the Denmark of *Hamlet:* ruled by a king with no right to rule, threatened by an outlying army, hoping for the rightful heir to rise up and take over.[15]

The Romantics cannot, however, take full credit for "discovering" the appeal of Shakespeare to Germans. Shakespeare began to become popular among German theatre artists in the late eighteenth century, though not all admirers of Shakespeare approached his works in the same way. In fact, the artistic experimentation in the German states in the late 1700s all but guaranteed that the reception of Shakespeare as an artist would be varied. Although the Romantic movement probably most directly led to Shakespeare's entrance into the German theatre tradition, the Classicists and the Sentimentalists viewed Shakespeare, or aspects of his work, as a model for their movements as well.[16]

Gotthold Lessing, important here as the earliest influential advocate of Shakespeare in Germany, argued that the contemporary theatre, as inherited from the rule-heavy Neoclassicism of Gottsched, was geared toward "Frenchifying the German stage, while ignoring the fact that German taste leans more naturally in the direction of England."[17] As dramaturg at the Hamburg National Theatre, Lessing created the *Hamburg Dramaturgy* in 1769, in which he invoked the influence of Aristotle. Although the French claimed to follow the guidelines of Aristotle, Lessing argued that their theatre was "in fact often founded on misapprehensions and distortions of Aristotle's ideas. . . . The English, unaffected in general by the pedantic French misreadings, have produced works both more vital and truer to the real spirit of the Greek theorist."[18] Lessing turned to Shakespeare as the ultimate example of English theatre and established him as the dramatist who would provide the best model for German playwrights.

Early in his career, Goethe also promoted Shakespeare on the German stage. Before his turn to classical principles, Goethe spearheaded the *Sturm und Drang* movement, which was heavily influenced by Shakespeare's dramatic form. In 1771, Goethe wrote the essay "On Shakespeare's Day," in which he posits Shakespeare as "the poet of nature, showing how humans are natural beings."[19] Goethe's essay praises Shakespeare beyond his poetry, comparing his own encounter with Shakespeare to "a blind man suddenly given the miraculous gift of sight."[20] He then wrote a defining Sturm und Drang drama, *Götz von Berlichingen.* The Sturm und Drang movement paved the way for the Romantic movement and theatre artists such as Tieck, but Goethe soon grew out of his Romantic tendencies, founded Weimar classicism, and lost his admiration for Shakespeare as a practical artist. In his early years at Weimar, Goethe included some of Shakespeare's plays in his repertoire, squeezing them into "classical straight jackets,"[21] but he eventually came to believe that, despite Shakespeare's genius as a writer, his plays were impossible to stage.[22]

In the same year as *Götz von Berlichingen,* Johann Gottfried Herder wrote an essay, "Shakespeare," in which he argues both that Shakespeare was a genius (a label the early Romantics did not bestow lightly) and that "each era and society creates its own dramas."[23] He accused the

French dramatists of "aping" Greek drama but falling far short of the ideal. A nation should create drama from "its own history, out of the spirit of the age, manners, opinions, language, national prejudices, traditions, and pastimes."[24] This, Herder argued, is what Shakespeare did. However, Herder continued, Shakesepare speaks not just to Englishmen but "teaches, moves, and cultivatesn*orthern men* [emphasis added],"[25] a geographical group that includes both the English and Germans. Shakespeare created drama based on his observations of and connection to Nature. Herder believed that, since the Germans have access to this same idea of Nature, Shakespeare speaks equally to them. Herder suggests that Shakespeare demonstrates an artistic freedom that he sets in contrast to Neoclassicism, which now "appear[s] an arbitrary imposition on German theatre by the aristocracy."[26] By the time Tieck was holding up Shakespeare as an artistic model, these theorists had embedded Shakespeare in a German artistic tradition as one who not only shares the essence of the Romantic spirit, but also of the German spirit.

The leap, then, from Shakespeare as admired dramatist to Shakespeare as promoter of German nationalism is not quite as far as it might at first seem. Based on the early Romantics' views of Shakespeare, he provided a model of theatre (both for the artists and the audience) that promoted national unity in two ways. First, it rejected the French model of Neoclassicism, thus ridding the stage of a damaging influence. Second, it gave the German audience dramatic material from an author whose spirit was the same as theirs. Audience members could now hear themes that spoke to their hearts, feel emotions that they had experienced themselves, and explore situations that might then affect their own decisions after leaving the theatre.

It was vitally important that the stage not only please the audience while they were in attendance, but that it also "combat mistaken systems of education" and give tools to the audience with which they could go out and improve their lives.[27] If the German nation was to succeed as a unified whole, the Romantics felt that its members must share a unified, collective presence, which included a call to Germans to do what was moral and right for themselves and for their nation. And, if the nation was to be founded on a cultural community, as the early Romantics hoped, the art must include not only nationalistic feeling but moral instruction. This is perhaps best exemplified by Friedrich Schiller's "The Stage Viewed as a Moral Institution."

As one of the founders of Weimar Classicism, Schiller is more aligned with the Classicist tradition than the Romantic movement, but his treatise provides a modified view of moral instruction from the typical idea of Neoclassical decorum. Many Romantics eventually adopted Schiller's ideas of the moral value of the theatre because of the emphasis on the choice of the individual. Whereas Neoclassical theatre, with its aim "to teach and delight," followed the rules so that there could be no question left to the audience to answer, the Romantic focus on the "inner man" gave the individual autonomy over his own moral decisions. The dramatist's main responsibility, according to Schiller, was to present material where "virtue and vice, joy and sorrow, are thoroughly displayed in a truthful and popular way."[28] As individuals of emotional and intellectual character, the audience members carried the responsibility of choice.

In his essay, Schiller highlights the importance of the theatre in a turbulent political climate, claiming that "the uncertain nature of political events . . . demands the stage as a moral force." His main argument for the stage is that, since "[s]ight is always more powerful to man than description," the condemnation of vice occurs more effectively using the visual medium of the stage rather than stated law. Schiller focused on more than just individual morality, however, and, like the Romantics that came after him, tied the theatre's importance into national themes. He called for a *permanent* theatre, one that "would have a great influence on the national temper and mind by helping the nation to agree in opinions and inclinations." He further called for the development of a *national* theatre as an important step in building the foundation of a unified Germany.[29]

Tieck's connection between art and morality is less straightforward than Schiller's outright proclamation. Still, his involvement in the Romantic movement, his connections to Catholicism, and his Herderian emphasis on the relationship of art to the audience of its time all suggest that Tieck was not simply interested in entertaining. He was not willing to present his audience with "German" art without providing guidelines with which to understand it. As a leader in the early Romantic movement, Tieck emphasized harmony with nature and the integrity of the human spirit (the emotional "inner man"). Though his religious views and spiritual feelings are difficult to establish, Tieck's early writings (particularly his contributions to *Outpourings of an Art-Loving Friar*, which he assisted Wilhelm Heinrich Wackenroder in completing) express a belief in a Catholicism to which he has been brought through art. The music and theatricality of the Mass elicit an emotional, spiritual response; Tieck "could not withstand the power which had been awakened in me."[30] Because the unity and spirituality of the Catholic faith appealed to Tieck, it is reasonable to assume that the moral teachings of the church found their way into Tieck's worldview. Most important, though, is the emphasis Tieck placed on art, the artist, and the reception by the audience (society) in the time the art was created. Tieck not only believed that studying poetry or drama within its original context would illuminate the time period of the art as well as information about the artist, but indeed he also posits a "strong, reciprocal connection . . . between the writer and his audience."[31] In other words, the reception of art by the audience, their demands and expectations, determine the art of the era. A necessary conclusion for Tieck's theory is that "a change in prevailing literary styles always indicates not only a new conception of beauty, but also a changing conception of morals and ethical values."[32] Therefore, the change in theatre supposedly instigated by the English Renaissance poets in fact would have been in part a creation demanded by the audience. The power here lies in the audience's ability to sway the artists to give them what they want.

The clear question that arises about Tieck's desire for and theorizing about Elizabethan practices is whether Tieck hoped to change the form of his contemporary theatre because he felt a "changing conception of morals" in his audience, or if he felt that by the process of changing the theatrical form he could create a new culture of morality, perhaps one akin to his view of the Elizabethan theatre, which he saw as "evolv[ing] 'naturally' from the common populace itself, bringing together all strata of society in [a] kind of theatrical community."[33] This idea mirrors Schiller's hope that in the theatre, "men of all ranks, zones, and conditions, set free from the bonds of convention and fashion, merge back into a single race, forgetting themselves and the world as they approach their heavenly source."[34] It is possible that Tieck felt he could instigate a change for the better in his audience by changing the theatrical form. If the created audience followed, they would be able to share in the instigation of something new and empowering, just as the Elizabethan audience did. It would be a self-affirming, creative process, resulting not only in new forms of theatre but in a new, unified audience.

Before turning to Tieck's insistence on Elizabethan practices, it is important to clarify that Tieck's Elizabethan productions would not necessarily be recognizable today as "original practices." The only Elizabethan production Tieck was able to mount was *A Midsummer Night's Dream* in 1843. It occurred in Potsdam's Court Theatre, which had a proscenium arch stage. Tieck found this type of theatre unacceptable for productions of Shakespeare. In writing about Elizabethan stages, particularly his novel *Der Junge Tischlermeister (The Young Master Carpenter),* he theorizes what his ideal stage should look like. The novel centers on a group of people—including a Baron, a professor, and a master carpenter—who make a journey into the country to produce a play. The Baron wants to perform *Götz von Berlichingen* and asks the master carpenter to build the stage. After performing and discussing the play, the group decides that "Goethe . . . was not a dramatist; he did not write for the stage at all."[35] At this point, the professor steps in and requests that they perform *Twelfth Night*—but not in the contemporary German manner. Instead, the professor suggests that, "if you want to bring out the harmonious unity of its components, to effect quick changes and to enable the actors to step forward and to recede into the background as occasion demands, you need a new stage, the stage of Shakespeare and his contemporaries."[36] So, the stage is rebuilt with the necessary changes, including widening the stage and reducing its depth, creating a raised inner stage and an upper terrace, and adding two staircases on either side of the inner stage that lead up to the terrace.

If this text is put "back into the context from which it was generated,"[37] the different social classes that make up the group become significant as they are working together to create what is essentially German literary theatre. The fact that Goethe becomes the unstageable playwright, whereas the production of Shakespeare with the new stage is a success, suggests that, in Tieck's view, even Goethe's contributions to German theatre did not help to create a theatrical experience that synthesized text and performance or that allowed the audience to relate to the performers. A production of a Shakespeare play is the only way to create this experience, but the play itself is not enough. The play must be staged using Elizabethan stage practices, the end result being a meaningful, uniquely German experience that is available to a new, class-diverse but unified audience.

Tieck's realized production of *Dream* in Potsdam satisfied his requirements for the inner stage and stairs leading up to a higher level, but the stage had to be built within the proscenium space that already existed, limiting the changes that could realistically be made to the stage. Many descriptions of Tieck's production emphasize his use of vertical space as opposed to horizontal. He achieved this effect in the proscenium Potsdam court theatre by having a structure built that created three playing levels connected by stairs on either side of the inner stage. These stairs appeared in most of Tieck's imaginings of the Elizabethan theatre. His inclusion of the vertical playing levels allowed him to "present the action with a fluidity unique to the time."[38] A large permanent backdrop represented the woods where the majority of the play takes place; the court scenes were represented in the foreground.[39] The mechanicals, however, did not have a specific area on stage to represent their work space, so a realistically rendered backdrop was lowered for their scenes.[40]

The vertical nature of the stage and the almost uninterrupted flow of performance it allowed make up the sum total of Tieck's realization of an Elizabethan stage. He still used realistically painted backgrounds, lowered columns onto the stage for the palace scenes, and included incidental music by Mendelssohn, which brought with it a ballet and a full orchestra to fill the pit in front of the stage.[41] While Tieck may not have been able to create his ideal Shakespeare performance as he realized it in his novel, *Der junge Tischlermeister*, he found a successful compromise between his vision and the audience's demands: the production "moved to Berlin and was performed a total of 169 times before being abandoned in 1885."[42]

Despite this production's shortcomings in terms of Elizabethan practices, the ultimate goal of an Elizabethan production as Tieck tried to realize it was an access to Shakespeare that would fulfill the Romantic desires for national unity and moral improvement. This access to Shakespeare is the key to Tieck's pursuit of the Elizabethan stage. If Tieck could produce a play closer to the way Shakespeare "intended" it, then he would allow the spirit (the "inner man") of Shakespeare, the very essence of Nature and Romanticism, to be more available to his audience. Tieck hoped to achieve this closeness not only through original practices, but also through assisting August Wilhelm Schlegel in new translations of Shakespeare's plays that claimed to allow German readers greater access to "the plays as they actually appeared in the First Folio, without omissions, contractions, and radical alterations that had marked all productions and publications of Shakespeare during the last decades of the eighteenth century."[43] With his theories on production and his translations, Tieck was in essence breaking through the patina with which contemporary theatre had covered Shakespeare in order to reveal what lay beneath. Through the use of more authentic texts and stage practices, Tieck's audiences would be able to experience more of a "true" Shakespeare, who, as a hero of (German) Romanticism, would aid them in their metamorphosis into an ideal German nation.

It is, of course, impossible to determine if Tieck's desires for his audience were realized. Germany did indeed become a unified nation, but it would be difficult to argue that Tieck's or even the Romantics' relationship to Shakespeare or their audiences had any direct effect on that event. It is also difficult to know if Tieck formed an "ideal" audience through a new art form, or if he was responding to an audience call for something new. One can assume at least that Tieck believed that the theatregoing public was ripe for the change. Whether the impetus came from the artists or from the audience, the unique aspect of both Tieck's and the German Romantics' mission to create an ideal audience is the focus on the content and form of the art rather than its national origin. Clearly, it was most important for the early Romantic artists, especially Tieck, to champion artists and their art based on the idea of a common spirit, a shared essence that could permeate the "inner man" of the audience members. The basis for a shared nationality was not what the Germans *had* created, but what they had the potential *to* create. Authors such as Shakespeare, forms such as Elizabethan theatre practices, in this sense took on a utilitarian role, training battalions of unified, moral German audience members who could march forth to create a nation based not on militarism and war but on a new German culture.

Notes

1. George L. Mosse, *The Culture of Western Europe: The Nineteenth and Twentieth Centuries* (Boulder, CO: Westview Press, 1988), 33.

2. I deliberately use the masculine pronouns because the trends I discuss here seem to be almost completely directed to the male receiver.

3. William Vaughan, *German Romantic Painting* (New Haven, CT: Yale University Press, 1994), 3.

4. Ibid., 3.

5. Mosse, *Culture,* 59.

6. Ibid., 55.

7. Friedrich Schiller, "The Stage as a Moral Institution," in *Dramatic Theory and Criticism: Greeks to Grotowski,* ed. Bernard Dukore (Boston: Thomson-Heinle, 1974), 445.

8. Mosse, *Culture,* 56.

9. Brian Vick, "The Origins of the German Volk: Cultural Purity and National Identity in Nineteenth-Century Germany," *German Studies Review* 26, no. 2 (May 2003): 242.

10. Mosse, *Culture,* 57.

11. Michael Perraudin, *Literature, the Volk, and Revolution in Mid-Nineteenth-Century Germany* (New York: Berghahn Books, 2000), 6.

12. Roger Paulin, *The Critical Reception of Shakespeare in Germany: 1682–1914* (Hildesheim: Olms, 2003), 254.

13. Ibid., 1.

14. Wilhelm Hortmann and Michael Hamburger, *Shakespeare on the German Stage: The Twentieth Century* (Cambridge: Cambridge University Press, 1998), 3.

15. Paulin, *Reception of Shakespeare,* 442–45.

16. See Simon Williams and Mark Hamburger, eds., *A History of German Theatre* (Cambridge: Cambridge University Press, 2008), for a discussion of the different movements in nineteenth-century German theatre.

17. Samuel L. Macey, "The Introduction of Shakespeare into Germany in the Second Half of the Eighteenth Century," *Eighteenth Century Studies* 5, no. 2 (Winter 1971–1972): 263.

18. Marvin Carlson, *Theories of the Theatre: A Historical and Critical Survey, from the Greeks to the Present* (Ithaca, NY: Cornell University Press, 1993), 168.

19. Simon Williams, "The Romantic Spirit in the German Theatre, 1790–1910," *A History of German Theatre,* ed. Simon Williams and Maik Hamburger (Cambridge: Cambridge University Press, 2008), 121.

20. Ibid., 121.

21. Macey, "Introduction of Shakespeare," 267.

22. Ulrich Suerbaum, "A Theatre for Shakespeare: The Early History of the Inner Stage Myth," in *Shakespeare: Text, Language, Criticism, Essays in Honour of Marvin Spevack* (Hildesham: Olms-Weidmann, 1987), 286.

23. Williams, "The Romantic Spirit," 122.

24. Johann Gottfried Herder, "Shakespeare," in *Selected Writings on Aesthetics,* trans. and ed. Gregory Moore (Princeton, NJ: Princeton University Press, 2006), 297.

25. Ibid., 299.

26. Williams, "The Romantic Spirit," 122.

27. Schiller, "Moral Institution," 440–45.

28. Ibid., 441.

29. Ibid.

30. Wilhelm Heinrich Wackenroder and Ludwig Tieck, *Outpourings of an Art-Loving Friar,* trans. and ed. Edward Mornin (New York: Frederick Ungar Publishing Co., 1975), 85.

31. Frauke Gries, "Two Critical Essays by Ludwig Tieck: On Literature and Its Sociological Aspects," *Monatshefte* 66, no. 2 (Summer 1974): 157.

32. Ibid., 162.

33. Michael Patterson, *The First German Theatre: Schiller, Goethe, Kleist and Büchner in Performance* (London: Routledge, 1990), 120.

34. Carlson, *Theories of the Theatre,* 174.

35. Suerbaum, "A Theatre for Shakespeare," 290.

36. Ibid., 290.

37. Dwight W. Hoover, "The New Historicism," *The History Teacher* 25, no. 3 (1992): 361.

38. Simon Williams. "The 'Shakespeare-Stage' in Nineteenth-Century Germany," in *Shakespeare and the Victorian Stage,* ed. Richard Foulkes (Cambridge: Cambridge University Press, 1986), 215.

39. Michael Patterson, "'Contributing Our Half': Ludwig Tieck's Shakespeare Productions in Dresden and Berlin, 1820–1843," in *The Globalization of Shakespeare in the Nineteenth Century* (Lewiston, NY: Edwin Mellon Press, 2003), 93.

40. Williams, "Shakespeare Stage," 215.

41. Gary Williams, *Our Moonlight Revels: A Midsummer Night's Dream in the Theatre* (Iowa City: University of Iowa Press, 1997), 105.

42. Ibid., 109.

43. Williams, "Shakespeare-Stage," 211.

Shuffling Roles

Alterations and Audiences in *Shuffle Along*

David S. Thompson

On May 23, 1921, a new musical opened in New York at Cort's 63rd Street Music Hall near the intersection with Broadway. While *Shuffle Along* was not the first show to feature an entirely African American cast, it has been hailed as the first to extend such a company to include the creators of the book and score while boasting an impressive roster of additional innovations. Perhaps most significantly from the perspective of the confluence of art and society, the score featured a non-burlesqued love song between an African American couple, a rarity for any venue at the time and the first such moment in a musical performed in a Broadway theatre.

Despite featuring a plot so paper thin as to be nearly transparent, the winding machinations of *Shuffle Along* proved overwhelmingly popular with audiences. The unlikely central premise concerns a pair of ne'er-do-well business partners who hatch a convoluted scheme to rig a mayoral election by running against one another in the hopes that the winner will appoint the loser to a position of prominence, thereby ensuring a favorable concentration of power in the city of Jimtown. Subplots feature a collection of crooks and cops, spouses and lovers in various comedic bits and musical interludes. The structure proved sturdy enough to support an additional assortment of vocal ensembles, musicians and dancers forming a lively and eclectic chorus. The resulting "musical mélange," as its creators termed it, proved popular enough to run for over five hundred performances in its initial Broadway run.[1]

The development and performance history of *Shuffle Along* contains many noteworthy features. The show paired two renowned vaudeville teams: musician-songwriters Nobel Sissle and Eubie Blake and comedians

Flournoy Miller and Aubrey Lyles. Typifying the swings of fortunes of the production, the collaborators found it necessary to chip in $1.25 each in order to afford the cost of treating a potential investor to lunch. Prior to bringing the show into New York, the two duos had amassed a debt of $1,800. However, brisk ticket sales and low operating costs quickly transformed the modest investment into receipts topping $1.4 million.[2] The score created a sensation in sheet music sales for many of its songs, but particularly for the signature tune "I'm Just Wild About Harry," a song that worked its way into nearly folk-song status through subsequent applications as varied as the Harry Truman presidential campaign and Warner Bros. cartoons. In addition to opening doors for Sissle and Blake as well as Miller and Lyles, it introduced several of its performers, including Florence Mills and Josephine Baker, to wider acclaim.

In the years that followed, but particularly during the remainder of the 1920s, *Shuffle Along* exerted tremendous influence, as one might readily understand the desire of producers to duplicate its financial formula. As a result, the production set styles of music, particularly for musical theatre songs, combining elements of ragtime, blues, and jazz. The ensuing decade also witnessed a vogue for African American shows, even if such productions simply used the style as a theme or starting point. The development of dance, especially tap, for Broadway performance also accelerated after the success of 1921.

Although one may measure success according to many standards, for theatre artists such standards must include the ability to reach an audience. Just as conversation may involve adjustments between message and feedback, reaching an audience may involve shifts in approach. The development of *Shuffle Along* represents three distinct relationships with the audience. The first phase offered a means of counteracting and subverting expectations of the time. The second phase attempted to change audience dynamics while shifting audience perceptions. The third reflected a moment of cultural exchange and expansion of influence.[3]

Vaudeville: Counteracting and Subverting

Even before the duo of Sissle and Blake met the team of Miller and Lyles, each pair had established an approach to their presentation and a relationship with the audience that served to counteract or subvert expectations. Rather than entirely embrace the lingering vestiges of minstrelsy or the images of Plantation life—staples of stage presentations in general and the Negro vaudeville circuit in particular well into the twentieth century—both acts found ways to alter the formula.

The more visible expression of difference belonged to Sissle and Blake, skilled musicians who created stage personas to reflect their ability. Although they became mainstays on the vaudeville circuit after World War I, their approach was shaped years before. Early in their careers, Noble Sissle had met the prominent musician and bandleader James Reece Europe. When Sissle persuaded Europe to find a job for his friend Eubie Blake, the pair had found a mentor. Europe dreamed of higher musical standards and a more respectful image for African American musicians, even imagining a black musical theatre.

Although Europe found little support for his theatrical vision, he created a sensation on the dance-band circuit, particularly after meeting the high-society dance team of Vernon and Irene Castle.[4] Europe's Society Orchestra displayed unparalleled musicianship and was the band of choice for two of the most fashionable white performers of the early twentieth century. Thus, the image of high style in upscale performances included an extremely visible group of ferociously talented and nattily attired black men. If Europe, and by extension Sissle and Blake, had not yet created a musical theatre for African Americans, they had managed to work within a parallel performance form to replace the negative stereotypes of a bygone era with a vastly more positive image.[5]

After a separation due to World War I, Sissle and Blake launched themselves into vaudeville, traveling around the country on the Keith circuit as the Dixie Duo.[6] Here, they remembered the image of their mentor. Combining that experience with the example of the team of Cole and Johnson, who had turned to vaudeville ten years earlier, Sissle and Blake dressed only in tuxedos and never performed in blackface. In fact, Sissle and Blake roundly rejected the suggestion of an agent who wanted to alter the act of the Dixie Duo. The agent had suggested that the pair don blackface and patched overalls and then discover, with no small amazement, a box with a piano in it. Sissle was to ask, "What's dat?" to which Blake was to reply "Dat's a py-anner!" before continuing with their act. They saw such a spectacle as tantamount to acting "like a couple of ignoramuses" and flatly refused the suggestion. In fact, their costuming took the opposite direction and their elegant attire became a trademark.[7]

By contrast, the comedy team of Flournoy Miller (1887–1971) and Aubrey Lyles (1884–1932) chose to work within the prevailing conventions. This is hardly surprising given their performance pedigrees. Lyles was from a well-known theatrical family: his father, H. H. Lyles, was a vaudeville veteran and a well-known black minstrel manager, and his mother, originally from Philadelphia, was one of the leading dance teachers of soft-shoe and buck-and-wing dancing. Miller, born near Nashville, also came from a family with a decided show-business bent: his brothers Irvin and Quintard also became entertainers. The two men met at Fisk

University and formed a partnership that led them into the Pekin Stock Company in Chicago as apprentice writers and actors. Such experience proved valuable since the Pekin boasted the first professional stock company in residence at a black theatre. While there, the duo developed a great deal of material that would provide a basis for their career. Most significantly, Miller and Lyles produced a string of musicals, including *The Mayor of Dixie* (1906), which would largely serve as the inspiration for *Shuffle Along*.[8] From the Pekin they graduated to the Keith vaudeville circuit, where they became an established team touring the United States and abroad. Irvin Miller declared, perhaps with a bit of bias for his brother, "They were the first Negro comedians who could do more than dance. They also succeeded as writers and actors."[9] Along the way, Miller and Lyles played many of the top theatres in the country, booked lucrative tours and also drew favorable comparisons to top acts of the day including Williams and Walker.

Perhaps owing to the influence of Lyles's father or perhaps due to their own initiation as performers in vaudeville houses, from the beginning Miller and Lyles found it necessary to "black up," adopting the burnt-cork convention of minstrel makeup. For nearly their entire partnership the pair worked within the confines of their audience's demands and expectations. However, while their look may have been typical, even stereotypical, their material set them apart. Miller and Lyles developed several routines that could easily be interpreted as either submissive or subversive, depending upon the audience. Variations in such reading would almost certainly fall along racial lines.

Arguably the most famous innovation of Miller and Lyles was the unfinished sentence routine. The routine is often associated with actor Mantan Moreland who used it in several of his films. Such an association has a solid foundation. Following the death of Aubrey Lyles from tuberculosis in 1932, Flournoy Miller teamed with Moreland. The new team began in vaudeville and then starred in a series of films featuring all African American casts, many of which were produced by Miller's production company. Of course, as with many a popular comedic routine, generations of performers adapted the concept and used it for their own purposes in the years that followed. The comedy arose from the technique of blending a series of innocuous statements and non sequiturs with interruptions, resulting in dialogue that walked the line between coherence and nonsense. Each performer would deliver just enough information to provide the outline of a story or situation, but interrupt before any individual reference became too specific. The result is the general sense of a conversation but with few details. Read dismissively, the routine is nothing but buffoonery since questions are never completed, answers are only suggested, and statements are left hanging. Audiences not identifying with the performers might well laugh with an air of condescension viewing a decidedly foreign mode of communication. The material also creates confusion for the listener and no small sense that the men possess an advantage in communication. While one may or may not conclude that they can read each other's thoughts, the tone of the exchange certainly foregrounds their connection, the fact that they understand each other and need not waste words to create the connection. In so doing, the performers create a conspiracy—a comedic conspiracy to be sure—but a conspiracy nonetheless. In such a setting, those who identify with the performers might ascribe a sort of power over words and thoughts or, more simply, appreciate the exchange as if they understood the password for admission to the club.

In citing such a reaction, we can draw upon fundamental semiotic principles of theatrical communication. Members of the audience initiate the communication event by their attendance at the performance, their willingness to engage in the exchange that unfolds providing a signal to the performers. For their part, the performers take advantage of the full range of vocal and physical gesture in order to heighten the effect of the performance by imbuing it with the highest possible communicative value. The resulting blend of linguistic, paralinguistic, and kinetic factors creates a particularly complex code. The means by which the audience frames the message or event contribute to the process of decoding the message.[10] Further augmenting the system under consideration, Susan Bennett notes that planning shapes perception of the event. For the purposes of analysis, planning would include such things as the location of the venue: a location designated as a Broadway theatre might indicate a different set of expectations than a vaudeville house, for example.[11] Thus, audiences from different backgrounds might well be expected to carry divergent interpretations of a presentation, particularly if their expectations of the theatrical event vary.

A similar range of reactions can be drawn from the so-called Figures Skit in which one of the performers offers a thinly veiled premise or problem requiring a calculation (e.g., dividing a restaurant check or distributing assigned tasks). The premise would then lead to a chalkboard demonstration of the equation $7 \times 13 = 28$ (Miller and Lyles also used the variation $6 \times 13 = 24$).[12] In brief, the comedy follows from the dramatic irony created by the liberal misuse of numerals in the "ones" and "tens" column of a number. The erstwhile mathematician, who claims truth for his erroneous equation, can be cast as either a dullard or a classic trickster. The latter interpretation rewards those who identify with the performers.

A physical analog appeared in the original version of *Shuffle Along* in the form of a routine imported from vaudeville, the "Jimtown Fisticuffs." In this comedic bout, an argument escalates toward violence, but never quite crosses the line. Instead, an elaborate dance of false aggression turns into choreography of advance and retreat until the moment of truth, when one of the combatants cannot take the tension any longer and runs away. Again, an audience could dismiss this as the behavior of silly cowards or the actions of clever men who lost nothing but lived to fight another day.

Joining Forces: New Models

As *Shuffle Along* opened at Cort's 63rd Street Theatre, the company found itself faced with what was surely an unenviable task at the time: appealing equally to black and white audiences. Tryouts on the road had proven that African Americans would respond favorably to the material, but success on Broadway hinged on building a following that crossed racial lines. As James Weldon Johnson noted, "the professional experience of Negro performers in New York had always been to play before audiences predominantly white."[13] Yet we must also consider that, for the predominantly white audience of 1921, it would have been a decade since they had seen an African American cast in a theatrical production in a Broadway house. Once again, the creative team both stretched the boundaries of the familiar and bucked trends in order to reach its audience.

A key aspect of the history of *Shuffle Along* involves ending a decade-long streak of few black performers on Broadway. Appraising the situation in *Black Manhattan*, his noted 1930 survey of the early twentieth-century conditions, James Weldon Johnson referred to the time roughly spanning the 1910s as "the term of exile."[14] The first decade of the century had given rise to productions such as *In Dahomey* (1903) and *Abyssinia* (1906). However, the era of successful shows featuring black performers quickly faded; by the time *Shuffle Along* opened in 1921, such endeavors were a dim memory. A combination of factors—including a political atmosphere that generally dampened race relations, a rise in segregation in the theatre and elsewhere, and a paucity of available theatres—meant that few entrepreneurs were willing to stake money on a black show.[15] Many black performers shifted their focus from theatre and adapted their talents for vaudeville.

The focus on vaudeville has particular bearing on *Shuffle Along*. From Tony Pastor's work in the 1880s, vaudeville impresarios sought to promote an atmosphere suitable for couples to spend an evening out.[16] In reality, promoters of variety entertainments walked both sides of the line, advertising entertainment suitable for mixed company but providing material racy enough to pique audiences' attention.[17] Good business frequently depended upon an important balance of delivering the vulgar while promising the wholesome and legitimate.[18]

Some skeptics were well aware of the vaudeville pedigree of the *Shuffle Along* creators and clung to the opinion that either performance venues had never cleaned up their act or that itinerant African American performers never would. In response, an advertisement for the show quoted a *New York Herald* review declaring, "The production is clean, and its humor more antiseptic than some regular Broadway shows."[19] A review in *Billboard* included the line, "Real, wholesome and filled with a spirit of liveliness and good humor." Eubie Blake summarized the situation: "We were afraid people would think it was a freak show and it wouldn't appeal to white people. Others thought that if it was a colored show it might be dirty. One man bought a front row seat for himself every night for a week. I'd noticed him—down in the pit you notice things in the audience—and finally, after the whole week was past, he came up and told me that now he could bring his wife and children because there was no foul language and not one double-entendre."[20]

Considering the appeal to white audiences returns us to the "term of exile" as described by Johnson. We should remember that his use of the phrase refers particularly to Broadway and that it somewhat ironically and possibly counterintuitively led to beneficial developments elsewhere. These included the emergence of stock companies, particularly in Harlem, as artists and managers promoted theatre by and for African Americans. In turn, the gathering of artists fostered collaboration among entertainers and allowed great stars to mentor younger performers, setting the stage for the emergence of popular black-themed shows in the 1920s, including *Shuffle Along*.

Another advancement to emerge from the "term of exile" was an attempt to broaden the features of black musical theatre in ways that had been considered impossible before. One show, *Darktown Follies* (1913), featured a love song performed sincerely and passionately by a tenor to his leading lady. That the moment became a hit with white audiences ran counter to the perceived taboo of expressions of love between African Americans on stage.[21] The love-song taboo had remained quite pernicious and as such impeded artistic expression and development. To quote Johnson again: "If anything approaching a love duet was introduced in a musical comedy, it had to be broadly burlesqued. The reason behind this taboo lay in the belief that a love scene between two Negroes could not strike a white audience except as ridiculous. The taboo existed in deference to the superiority stereotype that Negroes cannot be supposed to mate romantically, but do so in some sort of minstrel fashion or in some more primeval manner than white people."[22]

In addition to songs culled from their act, Sissle and Blake wrote a number of songs specifically for *Shuffle Along,* including "Love Will Find a Way" and "Everything Reminds Me of You," two numbers acted and sung as serious love duets. The composers expressed pride in these songs and they proved to be enormously successful, but they were performed with no small amount of concern. In an interview conducted years later, Noble Sissle, who, along with his co-creators, was also a performer in the show, confessed that they were particularly worried about the love songs: "On opening night in New York this song had us more worried than anything else in the show. We were afraid that when [romantic leads] Lottie Gee and Roger Matthews sang ["Love Will Find a Way"], we'd be run out of town. Miller, Lyles and I were standing near the exit door with one foot inside the theater and the other pointed north toward Harlem. We thought of Blake, stuck out there in front, leading the orchestra, his bald head would get the brunt of the tomatoes and the rotten eggs. Imagine our amazement when the song was not only beautifully received, but encored."[23] The material associated with the show met with broad approval. However, the company still felt it necessary to placate white audiences. Such strategies ranged from minor performance strategies to broader societal implications.

Performing without music scores, for example, was an old device, one that Sissle and Blake had learned from bandleader James Reece Europe. As Blake indicated to an interviewer, it was common practice for white bands to use sheet music on music stands, "but the people wanted to believe that Negros couldn't learn to read music but had a natural talent for it." In fact, the *Shuffle Along* pit orchestra was filled with talented musicians. In addition to reading music quite well, some were also handsomely augmenting their salaries in their off hours by creating arrangements for other musical groups.[24]

Of far greater significance is the role that *Shuffle Along* played in integrating Broadway houses. In some commentaries, it receives credit as the first production in a mainstream New York theatre to desegregate its audience. Yet even this moment does not arrive without caveats. Whereas blacks had customarily been restricted to the balcony, the critic for *Variety* noted with apparent surprise that "colored patrons were noticed as far front as the fifth row" on opening night. In fact, ticketing remained decidedly restricted. Two-thirds of the orchestra seating was available to whites only. *Variety* reassured its readers that "the two races are rarely intermingled."[25] Since this was a matter of box office management, one must assume that this decision came from the white theatre owners—the same individuals who had worked in tandem with Miller, Lyles, Sissle, and Blake to open the show.

While this section has concentrated on the appeal to white audiences associated with the Broadway run, all four of the creators of *Shuffle Along* proceeded with the avowed aim of producing a show that would entertain both blacks and whites. That meant including some of the staples of vaudeville blackness but steering clear of anything that might offend adherents of the New Negro Movement. Every song that utilized a bygone image was balanced by a romantic ballad or a production number that gently refuted the stereotype. As noted above, even the *attempt* to strike such a balance was not an enviable task.

In the case of appealing to black audiences, the results were mixed. Nearly every surviving account notes the overwhelming joy among members of the audiences, even among critics and commentators who did not care for the show personally. Langston Hughes cited the show as the beginning of the Harlem Renaissance and the primary reason for his decision to attend Columbia University.[26] James Weldon Johnson also suggested generally positive reactions.[27] Yet, prominent social activists could not agree. Writing in Alain Locke's *The New Negro,* novelist Jessie Fauset gushes for several pages about the attributes of the show.[28] In the same volume, dramatist and educator Montgomery Gregory categorizes *Shuffle Along* with "notable advances" in musical theatre, but then cites critic Ludwig Lewisohn, dismissing the show as self-caricature.[29]

Success: Expansion of Influence

The final point is a brief one. It would be a lovely completion of the thought if *Shuffle Along,* in addition to its other attributes and accomplishments, had done more to bring black and white audiences together. Since Broadway audiences of the era remained primarily white and Harlem entertainments primarily catered to black audiences, it would have been nice to see traffic move both uptown as well as downtown to witness the success of the show. However, such a demonstration would have required simultaneous productions in dual venues to prove the point, something far beyond the scope of the authors. It might also prove interesting if we could, if not erase or eliminate it, at least diminish somewhat the influence of locale as a nod to the ability of one group of artists and their creation to overcome perceived boundaries.[30] We do, at least, have the hint of a change in traffic patterns. During the "term of exile" in the 1910s, several significant productions attracted white audiences to Harlem. In 1913, the previously mentioned *Darktown Follies,* with its tender love song, saw its popularity spread downtown from Harlem, initiating "the nightly [white] migration to Harlem in search of entertainment."[31] Miller and Lyles attracted large audiences at the Hammerstein Theatre in 1910 and at a large book-musical featuring their comedic routines at Harlem's Lafayette Theatre in 1915.[32] Sissle and Blake frequently played the Cotton Club.

More directly relevant to this study, and in a move nearly unheard of at the time, a third touring company of *Shuffle Along* was organized at the Lafayette, opening on March 13, 1923. The next day, the *New York Amsterdam News* reported tremendous traffic and that "every seat in the theatre was occupied with standing room about six deep."[33] The glowing notices and subsequent success of the tour suggest broad audience appeal, echoing the sounds of the "migration to Harlem," which doubtless included more than a few downtown carriages heading uptown.

Separated by less than two years, yet linked by common material, the Broadway production and its Harlem counterpart brought audiences together for the same purpose: to see a remarkable "musical mélange" of an entertainment, hailed by audiences from a cultural cross-section and enjoyed regardless of venue. Combining this linkage with the associated acts of subversion and experimentation produces a picture of a single musical and the work of its creators. In turn, such a depiction represents a series of approaches to the audience relationship, running the gamut from simple survival to clever business, from testing social boundaries to encouraging social change.

Notes

1. Nearly every major source sets the number of performances at 504. Curiously, the Internet Broadway Database is the exception, listing 484 as the number. It appears, however, that the lower number does not take into account special midnight performances presented for the convenience of performers in other productions. These performances were numerous as various newspaper reports of increased traffic and pedestrian stargazing attest.

2. Robert Kimball and William Bolcom, *Reminiscing with Noble Sissle and Eubie Blake* (New York: Cooper Square, 1973), 88, 93.

3. This study draws from research included in the analytic chapter of the forthcoming critical volume *Eubie Blake and Noble Sissle: Shuffle Along,* edited by Rosalyn P. Schenbeck with consultants David S. Thompson, Constance Valis Hill, and Lawrence Schenbeck, published by A-R Editions, Inc., as part of the Music of the United States of America (MUSA) series. Research for the project is supported by the National Endowment for the Humanities as a project funded under the *We the People* initiative. This paper takes a different approach than that used in the critical edition, but considers some of the same material. Although it draws from my own contributions to the effort it is naturally informed by the

work of my collaborators. I am indebted to project leader Lyn Schenbeck for encouraging me to pursue this line of inquiry.

4. Marshall Stearns and Jean Stearns, *Jazz Dance* (New York: Da Capo, 1994), 95–98.

5. Kimball and Bolcom, *Reminiscing,* 58–63.

6. Al Rose, *Eubie Blake* (New York: MacMillan, 1983), 60–78.

7. Kimball and Bolcom, *Reminiscing,* 80.

8. Bernard L. Peterson Jr., *Profiles of African American Stage Performers and Theatre People, 1816–1960* (Westport, CT: Greenwood Press, 2001), 162–64, 184–85.

9. Stearns and Stearns, *Jazz Dance,* 132.

10. Kier Elam, *The Semiotics of Theatre and Drama* (New York: Routledge, 1988), 34, 78–79, 87–88.

11. Susan Bennett, *Theatre Audiences: A Theory of Production and Reception,* 2nd ed. (New York: Routledge, 1997), 125–27.

12. The Flournoy E. Miller Papers, Special Collections, The Robert W. Woodruff Library, Emory University, Atlanta, Georgia. The "Figures Skit" refers to a scene found among the papers of Flournoy Miller. The scene may have been inserted or rotated into the original performances of *Shuffle Along* featuring two of the lead characters. In the sketch Sam Peck tells Steve Sharper that, as one of seven men who raised twenty-eight dollars, he was entitled to his fair share, meaning one-seventh. However, through a series of ludicrous mathematical approaches Sam tries to convince Steve that one-seventh of twenty-eight equals thirteen. Sam demonstrates his point on a blackboard via multiplication, division and addition of a column of seven "13s." Many examples of the Figures Skit exist in film comedies. A search of YouTube using variations of the equation "7×13=28" will yield a lengthy list of clips. One available clip features a young Michael Jackson opposite comedian Flip Wilson on *The Flip Wilson Show.* The clip is notable because just after Flournoy Miller's death, his daughter sued Wilson and NBC for copyright infringement claiming that the material had appeared in a version of *Shuffle Along*. However, the sketch does not appear in the script for the 1921 version. A copyright search conducted in conjunction with the lawsuit could not verify that a printed version of the libretto containing the sketch existed. In exchange for dismissing all claims in the matter NBC settled the suit for $1,000.

13. James Weldon Johnson, *Black Manhattan* (New York: Knopf, 1930), 170.

14. Ibid., 170.

15. Thomas L. Riis, *Just Before Jazz* (Washington: Smithsonian Institution Press, 1989), 159–66.

16. David Walsh and Len Platt, *Musical Theatre and American Culture* (Westport, CT: Praeger, 2003), 18–21.

17. Andrew L. Erdman, *Blue Vaudeville: Sex, Morals and the Mass Marketing of Amusement, 1895–1915* (Jefferson, NC: McFarland, 2004).

18. Susan Kattwinkel, *Tony Pastor Presents: Afterpieces from the Vaudeville Stage* (Westport, CT: Greenwood Press, 1998), 1–7.

19. *New York Times,* May 30, 1921.

20. Kimball and Bolcom, *Reminiscing*, 94–95.
21. Johnson, *Manhattan*, 174.
22. Ibid., 171.
23. Kimball and Bolcom, *Reminiscing*, 93.
24. Rose, *Eubie Blake*, 59.
25. Allen L. Woll, *Black Musical Theatre: From Coontown to Dreamgirls* (New York: Da Capo, 1991), 72, quoting *Variety* for May 27 and December 9, 1921.
26. Langston Hughes, *The Big Sea* (New York: Hill and Wang, 1993), 223–24.
27. Johnson, *Manhattan*, 171–74.
28. Jessie Fauset, "The Gift of Laughter," in *The New Negro* (New York: Albert & Charles Boni, 1925), 165–66.
29. Montgomery Gregory, "The Drama of Negro Life," in *The New Negro* (New York: Albert & Charles Boni, 1925), 156. Thanks to my collaborator Lawrence Schenbeck for highlighting the reactions to *Shuffle Along* in *The New Negro*, both here and in the following note.
30. Susan Bennett, *Theatre Audiences*, 125–27.
31. Johnson, *Manhattan*, 174.
32. Peterson Jr., *Profiles*, 184–85.
33. "They're Off to a Great Start: Number Three Company of 'Shuffle Along' Scoring Big Hit," *New York Amsterdam News*, March 14, 1923.

When Audiences Attack

The Manhandling of Actress and Activist Kitty Marion

Christine Woodworth

ACTRESS and radical activist Kitty Marion wrote in her unpublished autobiography: "I have seen many tender, young plants by the wayside, in fields and woods, trying to struggle from under obstructions and removed the latter to give the former a chance to freedom of growth. By the same token, I want to see the removal of all obstructions in the shape of unjust statutes. Laws, rules, regulations, ordinances, theologies, dogmas and endless petty tyrannies which dominate, oppress, irritate, obstruct and curse the *spiritual* growth of humanity and, see our leaders, elected and otherwise living examples of what they want the rest of us to be."[1] Marion's revolt against "unjust statutes" fueled her work in labor campaigns, suffrage, and the birth control movement. Although her chief vocation was her work in the theatre—primarily as a music hall and pantomime performer—her most notorious performances were on the protest stage, placing her body on the front lines of the battles for the vote and access to birth control.

In the introduction to his watershed text *Performance Theory,* Richard Schechner notes, "Because performances are usually subjunctive, liminal, dangerous and duplicitous they are often hedged in with conventions and frames: ways of making the places, the participants, and the events somewhat safe."[2] Susan Bennett asserts in *Theatre Audiences* that performance theory has shifted the ways in which we examine audiences, noting that "the audience emerges as a tangibly active creator of the theatrical event."[3] Bennett goes on to ask, "Audiences clearly play a role in the theatre, but what kind of role? And what kind of audience? What constitutes the theatrical event in which they play that part? In what ways do the liminalities of performance bear upon the communication model of the performance itself?"[4] To these questions I would add: how might audience engagement with protest performance rupture frames and disrupt conventions, deliberately making protest performance unsafe? I will attempt to apply some of those questions to Kitty Marion's protest performances. Protest performances have their own sets of conventions, distinct from framed aesthetic performances, yet the parallels are clear. Protests, like many theatrical performances are action-oriented, spectacle-driven, thematically arranged, and provide deviation from daily life. One of the most pronounced differences between theatrical and protest performances, however, is the composition of the respective audiences. Presumably, audiences attending a traditional theatrical event willfully purchased tickets and planned to attend. Protest audiences are oftentimes much more disparate, comprised of fellow sympathizers to the cause, antagonistic opposition intent on staging a counterprotest, police or others responsible for maintaining order, individuals attending an event that was interrupted by the protest, or surprised onlookers. In the case of protest performances, the divisions between the performer (or protester) and audiences can be as varied as the composition of the crowd bearing witness to the event. The stakes are much higher for both performers and audiences in the realm of protest performance.

Barbara Green cautions against the tendencies of feminist historians to "collapse all versions of performative feminism under the umbrella term 'theater,' seeing pleasing pageantry and violent scenes of torture as elaborate performances that depend on the celebrity of female actresses."[5] Drawing clear distinctions between Marion's work as a professional performer on the stage and as a professional protestor in the streets, this paper will examine Marion's at times violent interactions with her protest "audiences." On several occasions, "audience" members who witnessed her protest performances broke the (admittedly porous) barrier between themselves and Marion. Specifically, this paper will explore those encounters between Marion and irate "audience" members that ruptured the safety of the frame and physically assaulted and/or forcibly removed Marion from the sites of performance. These instances of manhandling may be read on the surface as perilous disruptions of the frames and conventions of protest performances. Indeed, Marion did on many occasions suffer physically from these "audience" attacks. A deeper examination of these violent occurrences reveals, however, that Marion strategically narrativizes these incidents within her autobiography as a means of bolstering her cause. Likewise, journalistic accounts of some of these instances reveal the ways in which occurrences of manhandling have been used to depict Marion as heroic or to belittle her cause. It could be argued that these instances of manhandling are not in fact ruptures of the frame of protest performance but intrinsic to the "horizon of expectations" for political protest performance, which anticipate deliberate unsafety as a necessary convention. Thus, the success of a protest can partly be judged on the ways in which the audience members dismantle the walls between themselves and the protestors, sometimes through violence.

The early decades of the twentieth century marked a fervent period of feminist dissent in England and the United States. British suffragettes employed both creative and destructive modes of protest in their attempt to rally for the vote. Similarly, in the United States, early advocates of the birth control movement defied national and state laws to dispense birth control materials. Actress Kitty Marion was something of a nomadic figure, born in Germany and immigrating to England and then America. As a teenager she moved to England to live with an aunt due to turmoil in her home brought on by her emotionally and physically abusive father. Once in England, she quickly mastered the English language and soon pursued her dream of appearing on the stage. Her work in music halls and in pantomime was largely unremarkable, consisting primarily of chorus roles. Eventually, she was able to appear in small featured parts and as an understudy to principal performers. She made a living on the stage primarily through her work in provincial tours and later in long-running performances such as *The Lady Slavey* and *Kitty Grey*, for which she understudied the lead role. For Marion, as with many young performers, the tours were something of a turning point in social consciousness. As Julie Holledge writes in *Innocent Flowers: Women in the Edwardian Theatre*, "Touring the industrial cities of the North of England and Glasgow made a lasting impression on many young actresses, who had never seen slums or the effects of poverty before. For some . . . it was the beginning of a political awareness which led to their involvement in the women's rights movement."[6] Marion was no exception; she recounts in her autobiography that, during her times-off wherever she toured, she gravitated to the "poorest parts of the city."[7]

Marion's work in the music halls, specifically the challenges she faced in casting, also ignited her fierce quest for social justice. She was swiftly swept into public debates regarding the ways in which certain theatrical managers demanded sexual favors in return for bookings, highlighting her own violent run-in with an agent whose advances she spurned. Marion began active involvement in theatrical labor unions, specifically the Variety Artists' Federation (VAF) and the Actors' Association. She had long since recognized the gender disparity in the theatre. The VAF in particular, however, was resistant to taking on this cause. Marion's work within the labor unions led to her involvement with the British suffrage campaign. She joined the Women's Social and Political Union (WSPU), which had its own roots within the labor movement, and the Actresses' Franchise League. Marion was something of an anomaly within both organizations: most actresses that advocated for suffrage avoided the militancy of the movement, which the WSPU was especially noted for. Militant involvement was treacherous for actresses whose livelihood could be jeopardized by a night in prison and subsequent missed performances. Additionally, the Actresses' Franchise League did not want to forge alliances with any particular suffrage groups and thus attempted to maintain a semblance of political neutrality within the movement. Marion, however, was a self-proclaimed militant and boldly embraced the "Deeds, not words!" of the WSPU,[8] which Barbara Green labels "radical and audience-aggressive."[9] Martha Vicinus argues that "[t]he language, iconography, and ultimately the behavior of the W.S.P.U. portrayed an army at war with society."[10] Such descriptions cast Marion and her WSPU colleagues in antagonistic and sometimes dangerous relationships with those who witnessed the protest performances. While that was certainly the case for a number of their militant activities, Marion's interactions with her early suffrage protest audiences were not entirely violent.

Marion began her work with the WSPU by selling its magazine, *Votes for Women!*, in Piccadilly Circus. Eventually, however, she longed for a more active role in the campaign. Sophia A. van Wingerden claims in her study of the British suffrage campaign that the WSPU did not initially begin as a militant organization. Rather, in the early days it "confined itself to pursuing an anti-Government election policy, interrupting politicians at their meetings, and sending deputations to the House of Commons to see the Prime Minister."[11] Yet these events soon took a violent turn and Marion found herself in a situation in which the division between herself and her protest audience disappeared. Green's designation of the WSPU tactics as "audience-aggressive" can be read as antagonism directed at the audience by the protestors. Yet, in several instances, the peaceful protests of the suffragettes took a violent turn because of the aggressions of the audience. In her autobiography, Marion recounts her involvement in one parliamentary deputation:

> [Plain-clothes police who were] posing as a "hostile crowd" broke our ranks by shouldering in and pushing us away in every direction, and as each of us tried to proceed singly towards the House, petition in hand, two and three policemen, one on each side taking us by the arm and shoulder, quite unnecessarily pinching and bruising the soft under arm, with the third often pushing at the back, would run us along a little distance and fling us, causing most women to be thrown to the ground unless they were big and strong enough, like me, to kean [*sic*] well back while being run, and thus

> retain their balance. Many a small woman, I caught and prevented from falling, on this and other deputations, catching the ball, as it were, thrown by the police. . . . Aching in body and soul, I went home at last to find my arms and shoulders black and blue and painful, as were every woman's who had taken part in this rightful, legal, peaceful petitioning.[12]

The peaceful approach of the WSPU did not last long, however, as members soon resorted to violent activities including window smashing and arson. Marion herself notoriously set fire to the Hurst Park Race Course Grandstand. Marion felt compelled to participate in more militant activities upon hearing stories of her fellow suffragettes who had been jailed and undertook hunger strikes in protest. She wrote: "I called at Clements Inn, our [WSPU] headquarters, and expressed my indignation. Christabel Pankhurst gave me the opportunity of making my protest in 'deeds not words,' with a stone through a government window in Newcastle on Tyne, on October 9th, [1909] when Mr. Lloyd George would speak there on the budget, excluding women taxpayers from his meeting."[13] Accompanied by Dorothy Pethick, Marion threw a stone at a window of the General Post Office.[14] The first stone did not break the glass. She managed to hurl a second stone successfully just as one "audience" member—a policeman—grabbed her. Marion was hauled to jail, all the while yelling, "Votes for women!"[15]

It was in prison that Marion faced her most violent attacks yet. Marion, like many suffragettes as well as other political prisoners, launched hunger strikes as a means of protest during incarceration. The immediate audiences for such actions were fellow prisoners as well as prison staff. Secondarily, word spread outside the prison to journalists, supporters, and government officials. The death of a suffragette hunger-striker was undesirable for all involved so hunger strike protests were often met with violent forcible feedings to keep the protestor alive. Marion describes the act of forcible feeding in explicit detail in her autobiography:

> [Matrons] surrounded me and took me to the doctor's room, where three doctors, two in operating aprons awaited me. One asked me to drink some milk. I refused and was seized and over-powered by several wardresses, forced into an arm chair, covered with a sheet, each arm held to the arm of the chair by a wardress, two others holding my shoulders back, two more holding my knees down, a doctor holding my head back. . . . I struggled and screamed all the time. Not knowing the procedure of forcible feeding and thinking it was done through the mouth, I clenched my teeth when they had me in position and helpless, when suddenly I felt something penetrate my right nostril which seemed to cause my head to burst and eyes to bulge . . . Choking and retching as the tube was forced down to the stom-

> ach and the liquefied food poured in, most of which was vomited back especially when the tube was withdrawn. There are no words to describe the horrible revolting sensations. I must have lost consciousness for I found myself flat on the floor, not knowing how I got there. When wardresses were picking me up to carry me back to my cell, I heard one say "Eh, but she's heavy!" I said, "Of course, I am, put me down, I'll walk back, they would leave work like this for you women to do."[16]

The "audience" of prison workers involved in the forcible feedings ultimately altered the terms of the hunger strike performance by compulsorily putting an end to it. Yet the use of a feeding tube marked a new phase of the protest performance, thereby enabling Marion to reframe the prison worker "audience's" violent actions for her own ends. Marion, like many political prisoners who survived forcible feedings, used these instances as additional fodder for her cause, sharing her experiences countless times following her various prison terms as part of the suffrage movement's rhetorical strategy.

In spite of the horrors of forcible feedings, Marion continued her activist work in Britain. Indeed, as Martha Vicinus points out, "like the male denial of public space for political actions, the physical assault upon the prisoner's body only strengthened the resolve of the sufferer."[17] Marion found herself in and out of jail for the next few years. In prison, she continued her protests by ripping pages from the Bible, chewing the stuffing from her pillow, setting fire to her cell, and continuing her hunger strikes.[18] She was reputed to have endured 232 forcible feedings, some of which went horribly awry. In one particularly gruesome account, following an arrest for breaking the windows of the Silversmith's Association and Sainsbury's with a hammer, Marion wrote: "I decided not to struggle this time since I had been told how beneficial forcible feeding really is and how invalids and babies submit to it. There's the rub, 'submit.' In spirit, we were not going to 'submit' to forcible feeding any more than to disenfranchisement. Heart and soul revolted and resisted, but this time I would let the body submit."[19] The tube did not go where it was supposed to and Marion experienced excruciating pain. She couldn't stand up straight and couldn't take deep breaths. Ultimately, she was taken to the hospital ward.[20]

On another occasion: "the nasal tube, instead of going down, came out of my mouth and a throat tube was used, which was just as unpleasant and painful. The milk and egg they poured down was more and more curdled at each regurgitation. I lost weight rapidly and was released ten days later having struck two months off my sentence."[21] Even when "submitting" to the violent actions of her prison worker "audience," Marion found herself manhandled. Upon her release from prison in November 1909, Marion told the WSPU newspaper *Votes for Women,* "I am more than ever convinced of the necessity for militant action."[22]

Her activism subsequently took yet another turn, addressing not only suffrage but also the treatment of political prisoners. In her study of the strategic reproduction and dissemination of images of suffragettes being forcibly fed, Green argues that "the docile body produced through forcible feeding was *reproduced* in a distinctly modern way through the suffragettes' autobiographical narratives."[23] As Green writes:

> If pageantry turns on the pleasing display of the decorative body, the discourse of forcible feeding refuses the transparency of the visible, undoes femininity as a natural category, and transforms "experience" into a category of performance. Rather than giving onlookers a spectacular activism represented through marches and pageants, the discourse of forcible feedings gives us a series of uncanny reduplications as woman transcribes her "experience," each narrative constructed by the last and constructing the next. This is a form of feminist reproduction that takes over the work of duplication and circulation rather than staging a theatrical event for public consumption. Surveillance, the tool of containment and management for Foucault, is met by performance, creating the spectacle of the docile body.[24]

While Marion does, indeed, participate in the narrativizing of the "spectacle of the docile body," her experiences with forcible feeding constitute only part of her activist story. She repeatedly resuscitated those forcible feeding experiences, bringing them back out into the streets, reappropriating them in her fight against the very practice of the forcible feeding of political prisoners and thereby drawing in yet another layer of audience to witness her complex matrix of protest.

Marion endured a violent audience attack at one such protest. Attending a speech given by Lloyd George at the annual Welsh cultural festival in 1912, Marion interrupted him, yelling, "How dare you have political prisoners fed by force!"[25] She was subsequently thrown out of the hall and her clothing and hair were ripped to shreds by an angry mob. Marion recorded that her "hair was torn down, handfuls grabbed from every side, and pulled up by the roots."[26] In this instance, the audience present to hear George's speech quickly assumed the roles of aggressors in putting a violent end to Marion's interruption.

Not surprisingly, Marion's militancy ultimately had a detrimental effect on her theatrical career. One music hall agent allegedly told her, "If you take off those colors, I'll see that you get booked up for life." Marion, of course, refused, asserting, "No, you should have booked me before I put them on, it's too late to take them off now."[27] She was able to cobble together something of a theatrical career in between protests and incarcerations.[28] Eventually, however, she was forced to leave England at the start of the First World War because of her German birth. With the help of some of her suffrage compatriots, Marion was able to emigrate to the United States. Once there, however, her notorious militancy hampered her in a number of ways. She could not get work on the American stage because, "My connection with suffrage prejudiced some managers, who were most facetiously afraid I might smash their windows or burn the theatre."[29] Additionally, the American suffragists were wary of her militant past. Marion ultimately found work with Margaret Sanger, selling copies of the *Birth Control Review* on the streets of New York City.

Marion joined Sanger and others in Carnegie Hall on January 29, 1917, for a mass meeting, which served as the official launch of the *Birth Control Review* magazine and a public declaration of Sanger's battle for the legality of birth control. Sanger was in the midst of a trial for illegally operating a birth control clinic and her sister—Mrs. Ethel Byrne—remained in jail for her involvement. The meeting drew 3,000 attendees and the admission money collected was to be used to pay legal fees to fight birth control restrictions. The *New York Times* noted that there were women of all classes present and that "[m]any girls were in the audience who might have been high school students—few of them had escorts."[30] In a collision of causes, Marion found herself selling the *Review* with a former militant colleague. Marion wrote: "It was a glorious evening, reminiscent of defiant W.S.P.U. meetings. Mrs. Ethel Byrne was already in prison and hungerstriking. I, being interviewed by the Press, protested against her being forcibly fed, pointing out its result on my neck which had been getting worse lately, through the strain of unaccustomed physical work [house cleaning, etc.]."[31]

Marion continued her outspoken criticism of the practice of forcible feedings of political prisoners in New York. On March 7, 1917, she found herself back in Carnegie Hall. At a Civic Forum meeting, Commissioner of Corrections Burdette G. Lewis raised the issue of "so-called political offenders."[32] This protest resulted in Marion's ejection from the Hall, however, in a far less violent manner than her ejection from Lloyd George's speech years before. Marion described the evening in her autobiography: "'Why do you forcibly feed political prisoners' I called from the hall of the floor while Mr. Robert Lescher and a friend, both from Columbia, showered Birth Control leaflets from the gallery. The meeting, which had been listening very attentively to the Commissioner, was now electrified. Commissioner Lewis and I were developing an argument when the chairman Mr. Adolph Lewisahm intervened, saying I could speak when the program was finished, while at the same time a very large, imposing looking colored 'chucker-out' came to escort me to the door."[33] This instance, as well as the other instances in which Marion was "escorted" or removed bodily from her site of protest raise questions in terms of who from the audience is asked (or ordered) to rupture the boundaries between performer and audience. Marion never described an event in which a political figure touched her. Rather, the "audience" members that manhandled her were often in various states of disenfranchisement themselves due to their race, class, or occupation. Even in frame of protest performances, audiences remain stratified.

Marion's political determination in her new country was not swayed, however. She sold the *Birth Control Review* on the streets of New York—Harold Square, Times Square, in front of Grand Central Station, and on occasion on Coney Island—for thirteen years. Since Marion was unable to get on the American stage, selling the *Review* became, for a time, her sole source of income. While many applauded her for her work and eagerly (or clandestinely) purchased the *Review,* others angrily confronted her. Although it was perfectly legal for her to sell the *Review,* Marion was attacked and arrested several times. A 1927 *New Yorker* article somewhat whimsically remarked that Marion "has sold 86,478 copies, as of the first of August, we are informed, and all told has had much success and little trouble. Once an Irish lady engaged her in a one-sided fencing match with an umbrella, once some of Billy Sunday's followers denounced her publicly as immoral and upon one occasion the Vice Society had her arrested. She has come through each experience unscathed, however, and last month she even sold a copy of her magazine to a policeman."[34] The *Review* itself printed a number of stories on Marion's various arrests and at one point, launched a fund-raising campaign to help her pay the associated fines.[35]

Although Marion initially found it difficult to involve herself with the American suffrage movement due to her militant reputation, which followed her to New York, she did eventually find herself embroiled in a controversial suffrage protest with the Woman's Party outside of the White House on July 4, 1917. Throughout 1917, the Woman's Party's "Silent Sentinels" had been standing outside the gates of the White House and walking along Pennsylvania Avenue, in an effort to raise visibility for the cause and challenge President Wilson. Marion had evidently been working with the Woman's Party for sometime in Washington, DC, selling their newspaper *The Suffragist* on the streets in the weeks leading up to the protest.[36] As the paper itself noted in an article detailing the Independence Day incident, "Miss Kitty Marion, of New York, who for weeks has been selling *The Suffragist* on the capital streets without molestation, was attacked by a by-stander, who snatched her papers and tore one up. Miss Marion was arrested, as was her assailant, after her protest."[37]

Several pages of Marion's scrapbook, which is housed at the New York Public Library along with a draft of her unpublished autobiography, feature articles detailing this July 4 "attack."[38] The headlines of the stories often make the bias of a particular publication clear. While *The Suffragist* titles the story "Another Police Department Blunder," the *Washington Post* headline read "Militants in Riot; 13 Held for Trial,"[39] and a paper that Marion identified as the *Detroit Free Press* read "Suffs Stage a Comedy Riot." Evidently, one passerby, Charles Morgan, tore up a copy of *The Suffragist,* which Marion was selling as part of the White House protest. One paper attributed this to a "misunderstanding,"[40] claiming that Morgan thought Marion was giving away the paper. Another describes the event as an "altercation."[41] The *Washington Post,* however, describes the moment as a "knock down and drag out fight" in which Marion "delivered straight jabs, uppercuts and other fancy blows with the precision and force of a professional pugilist" necessitating the intervention of the police who "saved Morgan from a knockout." Marion was then arrested on charges of disorderly conduct and "bundled" into an automobile by the police. Standing up in the back of the car, Marion then allegedly "sang at the top of her lungs the 'Marseillaise' [which was] greeted with yells from the crowd."[42] Other members of the crowd, according to the *Washington Post,* "mussed-up" the suffragists and tore up some of their banners. The *Post* wrote a few days later that "Judge Mullowny dismissed [Marion] on her own personal recognizance, her future freedom to be contingent on her refraining from beating up mere men who may be disrespectful to the official publication of the 'cause.'"[43] Marion was honored for her participation in this protest at a Woman's Party meeting a few years later.[44] Though Marion's "altercation" with the disruptive audience member is shown in various lights depending on the publication reporting the act, the separation between audience and performer dissolved the moment that Morgan took the paper from Marion's hands.

Marion returned to New York and continued to sell the *Birth Control Review* until dismissed from her position in 1930. After a brief trip to London to witness the unveiling of a monument to Mrs. Pankhurst, she returned to her new homeland to face yet another bout of unemployment. Eventually, she was able to secure work with the WPA, helping children with their English pronunciation.

The instances of manhandling that have been outlined here are just a few of the occasions in which Kitty Marion placed herself in jeopardy in order to further her various causes. To a certain degree, her autobiography comprises a series of battles in her complexly interrelated fights for women's political and reproductive autonomy. Precisely why Marion created this autobiography remains uncertain, although Viv Gardner in her work on Marion offers a number of possibilities.[45] The reliability of autobiographies as evidence for theatre historians has been problematized by Thomas Postlewait.[46] What is certain, however, is that Marion depicted herself—and was often subsequently depicted by other activists and journalists of the time—as an unrelenting militant in the face of opposition. Marion's depictions of the "audience" attacks by police, prison wardresses and doctors, and oppositional bystanders (in one case, a little old lady with an umbrella) demonstrate the ways in which protest performances can be decidedly unsafe. The "audience" members that manhandled her were indeed "tangibly active creator[s] of the theatrical event" through the violence enacted on Marion's body and the unpredictable peril she was situated within. Surviving and narrativizing these incidents in the press and in her own autobiography enabled Marion to reframe these occurrences not as ruptures of the frames of protest performance but essential conventions therein.

Notes

1. Kitty Marion, Kitty Marion Papers. Manuscripts and Archives Division. The New York Public Library. Astor, Lenox, and Tilden Foundations, 71. It should be noted that the page numbering of the Marion papers is in a shambles. Pages numbers are skipped, page numbers are duplicated, and certain sections restart the pagination. I have listed the page numbers as marked on each page. However, there are multiple pages with the same number in vastly different segments of the autobiography.

2. Richard Schechner, *Performance Theory,* 2nd rev. ed. (New York: Routledge, 2003), xix.

3. Susan Bennett, *Theatre Audiences: A Theory of Production and Reception,* 2nd ed. (London: Routledge, 1997), 9.

4. Ibid., 17.

5. Barbara Green, "Advertising Feminism: Ornamental Bodies/Docile Bodies and the Discourse of Suffrage," in *Marketing Modernism: Self-Promotion, Canonization, Rereading,* ed. Kevin J. H. Dettmar and Stephen Watt (Ann Arbor: University of Michigan Press, 1996), 192.

6. Julie Holledge, *Innocent Flowers: Women in the Edwardian Theatre* (London: Virago, 1981), 15.

7. Ibid., 15.

8. Lisa Ticknor, *The Spectacle of Women: Imagery of the Suffrage Campaign, 1907–1914* (Chicago: University of Chicago Press, 1988), 8.

9. Green, "Advertising Feminism," 193. According to Green, "To Kitty Marion, militant activism was not just an alternative to the pleasing pageantry of the first half of the campaign, but a sign of its failure" (191).

10. Martha Vicinus, *Independent Women: Work and Community for Single Women, 1850–1920* (Chicago: University of Chicago Press, 1985), 261.

11. Sophia A. van Wingerden, *The Women's Suffrage Movement in Britain, 1866–1928* (New York: St. Martin's Press, 1999), 74.

12. Marion, 5.

13. Ibid., 14.

14. Estelle Sylvia Pankhurst, *The Suffragette: The History of the Women's Militant Suffrage Movement, 1905–1910* (New York: Sturgis and Walton Co., 1911), 448. Pankhurst writes that "Miss Dorothy Pethick and Miss Kitty Marion entered the General Post Office and having carefully selected a window in the neighborhood of which there was no one to be hurt they went out and cast their stones through it with a cry of Votes for Women."

15. Marion, 14.

16. Ibid., 22.

17. Vicinus, *Independent Women*, 271.

18. Marion, 24.

19. Ibid.

20. Ibid., 48.

21. Ibid., 52.

22. "Miss Kitty Marion Released," *Votes for Women*, November 19, 1909, 106.

23. Green, "Advertising Feminism," 193.

24. Ibid., 203.

25. Marion, 52.

26. Wendy Parkins, *Fashioning the Body Politic: Dress, Gender, Citizenship* (Oxford: Berg, 2002), 123.

27. Marion, 7.

28. Elizabeth Crawford, *The Women's Suffrage Movement: A Reference Guide, 1866–1928* (London: Routledge, 2001), 376.

29. Marion, 3.

30. "Mrs. Sanger Defies Courts Before 3,000," *New York Times*, January 30, 1917: 1.

31. Marion, 3–4.

32. "Woman Put Out of Carnegie Hall for Baiting Lewis," *New York Tribune*, March 8, 1917, 6.

33. Marion, 5–6.

34. "Malthus on Broadway," *New Yorker*, August 27, 1927: 12–13.

35. Margaret Sanger, "Kitty Marion Gives Up Freedom—What Will You Give?" *Birth Control Review*, November 1918: 4.

36. Inez Haynes Gilmore, *The Story of the Woman's Party* (New York: Harcourt Brace, 1921), 222.

37. "Another Police Blunder," *The Suffragist* 76, no. 5 (1917): 6.

38. It should be noted that Marion only occasionally identified the source of the clippings pasted in the scrapbook. Some are mislabeled. Attempts have been made to track down the original articles in their correct publications, wherever possible.

39. "Militants in Riot; 13 Held for Trial," *Washington Post*, July 5, 1917, 1.

40. Marion attributes the article "More Suffs Jailed Via White House" to *The Sun,* July 5, 1917.

41. Marion attributes the article "Suffs Stage a Comedy Riot" to the *Detroit Free Press,* July 5, 1917.

42. Marion attributes the article "More Suffs Jailed Via White House" to *The Sun,* July 5, 1917.

43. "Has Choice of Trial," *Washington Post,* July 8, 1917, 2.

44. "Many Women to Attend State Meeting," *New York Times,* February 7, 1921.

45. Viv Gardner, "The Three Nobodies: Autobiographical Strategies in the Work of Alma Ellerslie, Kitty Marion and Ina Rozant," in *Auto/Biography and Identity: Women, Theatre and Performance,* ed. Maggie B. Gale and Viv Gardner (Manchester: Manchester University Press, 2004).

46. Thomas Postlewait, "Theatre Autobiographies: Some Preliminary Concerns for the Theatre Historian," *Assaph C.* no. 16 (2000): 157–72.

Contributors

Susan Bennett is professor of English and associate dean (development and research) in the Faculty of Humanities at the University of Calgary. She is the author of *Performing Nostalgia: Shifting Shakespeare and the Contemporary Past* and *Theatre Audiences: A Theory of Production and Reception.* She also serves on the editorial board of *Theatre Journal.* Recent work includes a critical reading of the assumptions and practices of theatre history, focusing on the performance milieu outside London in the seventeenth century and how performance can inform editorial practices and other kinds of text-based analysis.

Jane Barnette, resident dramaturg of the Department of Theatre, Performance Studies, and Dance at Kennesaw State University, is a theatre historian who does archival research on train culture and American pageantry. She serves as the regional vice president of the Literary Managers and Dramaturgs of America (LMDA) and has been published in *Theatre Symposium, Theatre Journal,* and *Text & Performance Quarterly.*

Becky Becker, associate professor of theatre and head of the BA program, teaches courses in theatre history, script analysis, playwriting, and devising performance at Columbus State University in Columbus, Georgia. Her directing credits include *The Conduct of Life, Once on This Island, A Midsummer Night's Dream, The Laramie Project, Cloud Nine,* and *Eurydice.* She has also conceived and directed several oral history performances, including *Westville: Collected Lives,* describing the founding of a historic 1850s village in Georgia, and *Bibb City: Collected Lives from a Mill Town,* chronicling mill life on the Chattahoochee River. Becky's published work may be found in *Theatre Journal, Feminist Teacher,* and *Theatre Symposium.*

Lisa Bernd teaches dramatic literature, theory, and criticism at Cleveland State University in Ohio. After receiving her PhD in theatre from the University of Wisconsin–Madison, she held a research fellowship at the University of Warsaw in Poland and taught at the University of Oklahoma in Norman. She has published articles and reviews in *Theatre Journal, Text and Presentation,* and *The Baylor Journal of Theatre.* Her research interests include the representation of national and ethnic identity, feminist theory and pedagogy, and the history of popular entertainment in the twentieth century. She is especially interested in the relationship between the theatre and communal identity. She studies and writes about Polish national theatre, Native American theatre, theatre about the Holocaust, and the representation of American nationalism in Wild West shows.

Evan Bridenstine is asociate professor of theatre at Methodist University in Fayetteville, North Carolina, where he has taught since 2001. He holds an MA from Kent State University, an MFA in playwriting from the University of Virginia, and a PhD from the Ohio State University.

Michael Jaros is assistant professor of English at Salem State University in Salem, Massachusetts. He received his PhD in drama and theatre from the University of California, San Diego, in June 2008, where he worked as a dramaturg in the professional theatre training program as well as at the San Diego Repertory Theatre. His research focuses on twentieth-century Irish culture in performance; he has authored several articles on the subject. He also holds an MPhil from Trinity College, Dublin, in Irish theatre and film and an MA in theatre history from the University of Texas at Austin.

Robert I. Lublin is chair of the Department of Performing Arts at the University of Massachusetts–Boston. His forthcoming book is *Costuming the Shakespearean Stage: Visual Codes of Representation in Early Modern Theatre and Culture.* He is also coediting a collection of essays on modern adaptations and appropriations of Shakespeare to be published by Palgrave.

Paulette Marty received her MA in Renaissance drama from the University of Warwick in the UK and her PhD from the University of Wisconsin-Madison. She teaches theatre history and play analysis at Appalachian State University where she also serves as the faculty coordinator of general education.

Natalie Tenner is a PhD candidate at the University of Maryland where she studies Elizabethan-style productions of Shakespeare in nineteenth-century Germany and England. She received her MA in English from the University of Warwick. She is the resident dramaturg for Odd Act Theatre Group and has acted as dramaturg for productions at the University of Maryland and Chesapeake Shakespeare Company.

David S. Thompson is the Annie Louise Harrison Waterman Professor of Theatre at Agnes Scott College in Atlanta. He has published numerous articles in the popular press concerning trends in Broadway performance and theatrical awards. He is preparing the critical edition of the landmark musical *Shuffle Along* for publication under the guidance of his coauthors Lyn and Larry Schenbeck. Thompson is a past president of the Southeastern Theatre Conference, the parent organization of Theatre Symposium.

Christine Woodworth teaches theatre history and feminist theatre and serves as resident dramaturg at UNC–Greensboro where she is also a cross-appointed faculty member in the Women's and Gender Studies Program. Her articles and reviews have appeared in *Theatre Annual, Text and Presentation, Theatre Topics, Theatre Journal,* and *Theatre Symposium.* She is currently at work on the intersection of theatre and reproductive politics and has two forthcoming essays on that topic: "Back-Alleys to Basements: Narratives of Class and (Il)legal Abortion on the American Stage" in *To Have or Have Not: Essays on Commerce and Capital in Modernist Theatre* (edited by James Fisher) and "Playing Missionary in Harlem?: Race, Public Policy, and Birth Control Crusaders in the Harlem Renaissance" in *Public Theatres and Theatre Publics* (edited by Robert Shimko and Sara Freeman).

Cover Illustration: G. Durand, engraving, "Saturday Night at the Victoria Theatre," *The Graphic* [London], October 26, 1872, 152. Public Domain.

THEATRE SYMPOSIUM (ISSN 1065-4917) is published annually by The University of Alabama Press, Box 870380, Tuscaloosa, AL 35487-0380. Subscription rates for 2012 are $25.00 for individuals, $30.00 for institutions, and $38.00 for foreign. Back issues are $25.00.

Paperback ISBN 978-0-8173-7007-7
eBook ISBN: 978-0-8173-8632-0